# SQL

## *Beginner to Pro Guide*

By

Timothy Short

© **Copyright 2016 by DCB Web Trading Ltd**_____ -
**All rights reserved.**

This document is geared towards providing exact and reliable information in regards to the topic and issue covered. The publication is sold with the idea that the publisher is not required to render accounting, officially permitted, or otherwise, qualified services. If advice is necessary, legal or professional, a practiced individual in the profession should be ordered.

- From a Declaration of Principles which was accepted and approved equally by a Committee of the American Bar Association and a Committee of Publishers and Associations.

In no way is it legal to reproduce, duplicate, or transmit any part of this document in either electronic means or in printed format. Recording of this publication is strictly prohibited and any storage of this document is not allowed unless with written permission from the publisher. All rights reserved.

The information provided herein is stated to be truthful and consistent, in that any liability, in terms of inattention or otherwise, by any usage or abuse of any policies, processes, or directions contained within is the solitary and utter responsibility of the recipient reader. Under no circumstances will any legal responsibility or blame be held against the publisher for any reparation, damages, or monetary loss due to the information herein, either directly or indirectly.

Respective authors own all copyrights not held by the publisher.

The information herein is offered for informational purposes solely, and is universal as so. The presentation of the information is without contract or any type of guarantee assurance.

The trademarks that are used are without any consent, and the publication of the trademark is without permission or backing by the trademark owner. All trademarks and brands within this book are for clarifying purposes only and are the owned by the owners themselves, not affiliated with this document.

# Table of Contents

Introduction ..................................................................................................1
Chapter 1: What is SQL?..............................................................................3
Chapter 2: Introduction to SQL ....................................................................5
Chapter 3: SQL Syntax .................................................................................7
Chapter 4: SQL Select ................................................................................10
Chapter 5: SQL Distinct .............................................................................13
Chapter 6: SQL Where ...............................................................................15
Chapter 7: SQL And / Or............................................................................18
Chapter 8: SQL Order By ...........................................................................21
Chapter 9: SQL Insert Into .........................................................................25
Chapter 10: SQL Update ............................................................................29
Chapter 11: SQL Delete .............................................................................32
Chapter 12: SQL Injection..........................................................................35
Chapter 13: SQL Select Top.......................................................................40
Chapter 14: SQL Like ................................................................................43
Chapter 15: SQL Wildcards .......................................................................47
Chapter 16: SQL In ....................................................................................51
Chapter 17: SQL Between..........................................................................54
Chapter 18: SQL Aliases ............................................................................58
Chapter 19: SQL Joins................................................................................62
Chapter 20: SQL Inner Join........................................................................65
Chapter 21: SQL Left Join .........................................................................68
Chapter 22: SQL Right Join .......................................................................71
Chapter 23: SQL Full Join..........................................................................74
Chapter 24: SQL Union..............................................................................76
Chapter 25: SQL Select Into.......................................................................80
Chapter 26: SQL Insert Into Select ............................................................83

Chapter 27: SQL Create DB ............................................................... 86
Chapter 28: SQL Create Table ............................................................ 88
Chapter 29: SQL Constraints .............................................................. 91
Chapter 30: SQL Not Null .................................................................. 93
Chapter 31: SQL Unique .................................................................... 95
Chapter 32: SQL Primary Key ............................................................ 98
Chapter 33: SQL Foreign Key ........................................................... 101
Chapter 34: SQL Check .................................................................... 105
Chapter 35: SQL Default .................................................................. 108
Chapter 36: SQL Create Index .......................................................... 111
Chapter 37: SQL Drop ...................................................................... 113
Chapter 38: SQL Alter ...................................................................... 115
Chapter 39: SQL Auto Increment ...................................................... 118
Chapter 40: SQL Views .................................................................... 122
Chapter 41: SQL Dates ..................................................................... 125
Chapter 42: SQL Null Values ........................................................... 129
Chapter 43: SQL Null Functions ...................................................... 132
Chapter 44: SQL Data Types ............................................................ 135
Chapter 45: SQL DB Data Types ...................................................... 138
Conclusion ........................................................................................ 146
Other Books by Timothy Short .......................................................... 148

# Introduction

I want to thank you and congratulate you for choosing the book, *"**SQL: Beginner to Pro Guide**"*.

This book contains proven steps and strategies on how to become a pro at the use of SQL programming!

Whether you are a beginner, already have your feet in the water of SQL programming, or are a seasoned veteran, this step-by-step guide is sure to have something for you.

You will learn everything from what SQL is, the benefits of programming with SQL, programming at the most basic levels, all the way to how to program like a pro. If you are using SQL for your website, then you will be especially interested in how to properly program to prevent malicious hackers from destroying your database with an SQL injection! Don't know what that is? Well, it's nasty and we can show you how to prevent it.

This book includes everything from SQL SELECT to SQL WILDCARDS, and even how to create your own database and recommended data types, and everything in between!

Thanks again for choosing this book, I hope you enjoy it!

# Chapter 1: What is SQL?

Structured Query Language, or SQL, is a specialized programming language used for managing data in an RDBMS, Relational Database Management System, or for stream processing in an RDSMS, Relational Data Stream Management System.

SQL is an American National Standards Institute, or ANSI, standard language used to allow you to access and manipulate databases.

This allows you to access and change databases containing information on people, products, order history, and pretty much anything else used by many dynamic websites across the World Wide Web.

# Chapter 2: Introduction to SQL

Here is a short list of what you can do using SQL and databases:

> Execute queries against a database
- Collect data from a database
- Insert, update and delete records in databases
- Create whole new databases
- Create entirely new tables within an existing database
- Create and store procedures within a database
- Create views within a database
- Set permissions on tables, procedures and views in a database

Even though SQL is an ANSI standard, there are variations throughout the industry. However, in order to comply with ANSI, they all support major commands, such as Update, Delete, Insert, Select, and Where.

In order to build a website that shows information from a database, you will need the following:

- An RDBMS program like SQL Server, MySQL, or MS Access.
- Use server side scripting like PHP or ASP
- Use SQL to obtain the data you want
- Use HTML/CSS

**What is RDBMS?**

Relational Database Management Systems are the basis for SQL, as well as all modern database systems, like IMB DB2, MS SQL Server, Oracle, Microsoft Access, and MySQL.

The data contained within an RDBMS is stored in what is called tables, which are collections of related data placed in columns and rows.

# Chapter 3: SQL Syntax

Databases often contain more than one table. Each table has its own name. The rows in a table are known as records, whereas the columns contain data for each record. Throughout the tutorials you will see here, we will be working with the Northwind sample database. This is included in MS SQL Server and MS Access. Below you will find a selection from the table named "Customers."

| CustomerID | CustomerName | Contact Name | Address | City | PostalCode | Country |
|---|---|---|---|---|---|---|
| 1 | Alfreds Futterkiste | Maria Anders | Obere Str. 57 | Berlin | 12209 | Germany |
| 2 | Ana Trujillo Emparedados y helados | Ana Trujillo | Avda. de la Constitución 2222 | México D.F. | 05021 | Mexico |
| 3 | Antonio Moreno Taquería | Antonio Moreno | Mataderos 2312 | México D.F. | 05023 | Mexico |
| 4 | Around the Horn | Thomas Hardy | 120 Hanover Sq. | London | WA1 1DP | UK |
| 5 | Berglunds snabbköp | Christina Berglund | Berguvsvägen 8 | Luleå | S-958 22 | Sweden |

(The above table from the Northwind sample database contains five records (rows) and seven columns. Each record pertains to one customer, and each column pertains to data on that customer.)

**Statements**

Most actions performed on a database are done by utilizing SQL Statements. In order to select all records in the "Customers" table, use the following statement:

*SELECT * FROM Customers;*

When doing this, you will see that rather than just 5 rows, you get the complete list of customers in the table.

SQL keywords are not case sensitive, that means that *SELECT* = *select* = *Select*.

However, for the sake of continuity, we will use all uppercase for all SQL keywords.

**Semicolon Usage:**

The use of a semicolon at the end of each SQL statement is required by some database systems. This is the standard practice for separating each SQL statement when the database system allows more than one statement to be executed in the same server call. We will be using a semicolon at the end of each statement.

**Important and Common SQL Commands:**

**SELECT** - extract database data

**UPDATE** - updates database data

**DELETE** - deletes database data

**INSERT INTO** - inserts new database data

**CREATE DATABASE** - creates new database

**ALTER DATABASE** - modifies database

**CREATE TABLE** - creates a table

**ALTER TABLE** - modifies a table

**DROP TABLE** – removes or deletes a table

**CREATE INDEX** - creates search key or index

**DROP INDEX** - deletes index

# Chapter 4: SQL Select

The SQL SELECT Statement is used to extract data from a database. Once used, you will see the results displayed in what is called a result-set, or a result table.

SQL SELECT Syntax:

*SELECT column_name,column_name*

*FROM table_name;*

And

*SELECT * FROM table_name;*

Again, we are using the Northwind sample database. Below is a selection of Northwind's "Customers" table:

| CustomerID | CustomerName | Contact Name | Address | City | PostalCode | Country |
|---|---|---|---|---|---|---|
| 1 | Alfreds Futterkiste | Maria Anders | Obere Str. 57 | Berlin | 12209 | Germany |
| 2 | Ana Trujillo Emparedados y helados | Ana Trujillo | Avda. de la Constitución 2222 | México D.F. | 05021 | Mexico |
| 3 | Antonio Moreno Taqueria | Antonio Moreno | Mataderos 2312 | México D.F. | 05023 | Mexico |
| 4 | Around the Horn | Thomas Hardy | 120 Hanover Sq. | London | WA1 1DP | UK |
| 5 | Berglunds snabbköp | Christina Berglund | Berguvsvägen 8 | Luleå | S-958 22 | Sweden |

The following is an example of selecting columns. This SQL Statement selects the "CustomerName" and "City" columns:

*SELECT CustomerName,City FROM Customers;*

Number of Records: 91

| CustomerName | City |
|---|---|
| Alfreds Futterkiste | Berlin |
| Ana Trujillo Emparedados y helados | México D.F. |
| Antonio Moreno Taqueria | México D.F. |
| Around the Horn | London |
| Berglunds snabbköp | Luleå |

(This example only contains the first five cities that would be listed in the Northwind sample database.)

Using this statement will provide you with a results table containing a complete list of all customers in one column, and their cities in the other.

Alternately, as seen before, you can select all columns in the table titled "Customers" by using this statement:

*SELECT \* FROM Customers;*

**Navigating in a Result Table**

Navigation in the result-set with programming functions is allowed in most database software systems. Such programming functions include Get-Record-Content, Move-To-First-Record, Move-To-Next-Record, etc.

# Chapter 5: SQL Distinct

The SQL SELECT DISTINCT statement returns only different or distinct values.

Duplicate values may be contained within columns on a table, and occasionally you will only want to show different values with no duplicates.

SQL DISTINCT syntax:

*SELECT DISTINCT column_name,column_name*

*FROM table_name;*

**Example:**

Using the following statement will return a complete list of all cities, with no duplicates, from column titled "City" of the table titled "Customers":

*SELECT DISTINCT City FROM Customers;*

| City |
|---|
| Berlin |
| México D.F. |
| London |
| Luleå |
| Mannheim |

This example only contains the first five cities that would be listed in the Northwind sample database.

# Chapter 6: SQL Where

The SQL WHERE clause is used as a filter, in order to extract only records that fulfill the criteria specified.

SQL WHERE Syntax:

> SELECT column_name,column_name
>
> FROM table_name
>
> WHERE column_name operator value;

**Example:**

Using the following statement will return a result-set containing all customer from "Mexico" within the "Customers" table:

> SELECT * FROM Customers
>
> WHERE Country='Mexico';

Number of Records: 5

| CustomerID | CustomerName | ContactName | Address | City | PostalCode | Country |
| --- | --- | --- | --- | --- | --- | --- |
| 2 | Ana Trujillo Emparedados y helados | Ana Trujillo | Avda. de la Constitución 2222 | México D.F. | 05021 | Mexico |
| 3 | Antonio Moreno Taquería | Antonio Moreno | Mataderos 2312 | México D.F. | 05023 | Mexico |
| 13 | Centro comercial Moctezuma | Francisco Chang | Sierras de Granada 9993 | México D.F. | 05022 | Mexico |
| 58 | Pericles Comidas clásicas | Guillermo Fernández | Calle Dr. Jorge Cash 321 | México D.F. | 05033 | Mexico |
| 80 | Tortuga Restaurante | Miguel Angel Paolino | Avda. Azteca 123 | México D.F. | 05033 | Mexico |

Typically, SQL requires that text values have single quotes around them, and most allow double quotes. Alternately, numeric values should not have quotes.

# Example:

SELECT * FROM Customers
WHERE CustomerID=1;

Number of Records: 1

| CustomerID | CustomerName | Contact Name | Address | City | PostalCode | Country |
|---|---|---|---|---|---|---|
| 1 | Alfreds Futterkiste | Maria Anders | Obere Str. 57 | Berlin | 12209 | Germany |

## Operators:

Here is a list of operators that can be used in the WHERE clause:

| Operator | Description |
|---|---|
| = | Equal |
| <> | Not equal. In some versions of SQL, it can also be written as != |
| > | Greater than |
| < | Less than |
| >= | Greater than or equal |
| <= | Less than or equal |
| BETWEEN | Between an inclusive range |
| LIKE | Search for a pattern |
| IN | To specify multiple possible values for a column |

# Chapter 7: SQL And / Or

Both the AND and OR operators filter records based on multiple criteria. The AND operator displays data based on the first condition as well as the second condition stated if both conditions are true. The OR operator displays data of the first condition or the second condition if either condition is true.

**AND Example:**

The following statement selects customer from the country of "Germany" and the city of "Berlin":

> SELECT * FROM Customers
>
> WHERE Country='Germany'
>
> AND City='Berlin';

Number of Records: 1

| CustomerID | CustomerName | Contact Name | Address | City | PostalCode | Country |
|---|---|---|---|---|---|---|
| 1 | Alfreds Futterkiste | Maria Anders | Obere Str. 57 | Berlin | 12209 | Germany |

**OR Example:**

> SELECT * FROM Customers
>
> WHERE City='Berlin'
>
> OR City='München';

Number of Records: 2

| CustomerID | CustomerName | Contact Name | Address | City | PostalCode | Country |
|---|---|---|---|---|---|---|
| 1 | Alfreds Futterkiste | Maria Anders | Obere Str. 57 | Berlin | 12209 | Germany |
| 25 | Frankenversand | Peter Franken | Berliner Platz 43 | München | 80805 | Germany |

**Using AND and OR together**

You can use parenthesis to form more complex expressions to combine operators, such as AND and OR.

**AND and OR example:**

The following statement customers from the country of "Germany" and city of "Berlin" or city of "Munchn" in the "Customers" table:

> *SELECT \* FROM Customers*
>
> *WHERE Country='Germany'*
>
> *AND (City='Berlin' OR City='München');*

Number of Records: 2

| CustomerID | CustomerName | Contact Name | Address | City | PostalCode | Country |
|---|---|---|---|---|---|---|
| 1 | Alfreds Futterkiste | Maria Anders | Obere Str. 57 | Berlin | 12209 | Germany |
| 25 | Frankenversand | Peter Franken | Berliner Platz 43 | München | 80805 | Germany |

# Chapter 8: SQL Order By

The SQL ORDER BY keyword is used in order to sort a result-set or result table by one or multiple columns. For example, using DESC will sort the data into descending order.

SQL ORDER BY syntax:

>SELECT column_name, column_name
>
>FROM table_name
>
>ORDER BY column_name ASC|DESC, column_name ASC|DESC;

**Example:**

The following SQL statement will select all customers and order the result table by the "Country" column.

>SELECT * FROM Customers
>
>ORDER BY Country;

Number of Records: 91

| CustomerID | CustomerName | Contact Name | Address | City | PostalCode | Country |
|---|---|---|---|---|---|---|
| 12 | Cactus Comidas para llevar | Patricio Simpson | Cerrito 333 | Buenos Aires | 1010 | Argentina |
| 54 | Océano Atlántico Ltda. | Yvonne Moncada | Ing. Gustavo Moncada 8585 Piso 20-A | Buenos Aires | 1010 | Argentina |
| 64 | Rancho grande | Sergio Gutiérrez | Av. del Libertador 900 | Buenos Aires | 1010 | Argentina |
| 20 | Ernst Handel | Roland Mendel | Kirchgasse 6 | Graz | 8010 | Austria |
| 59 | Piccolo und mehr | Georg Pipps | Geislweg 14 | Salzburg | 5020 | Austria |

(This example only contains the first five ordered by country that would be listed in the Northwind sample database.)

**DESC Example:**

The following SQL statement does the same as above, however in descending order.

> SELECT * FROM Customers
>
> ORDER BY Country DESC;

Number of Records: 91

| CustomerID | CustomerName | ContactName | Address | City | PostalCode | Country |
|---|---|---|---|---|---|---|
| 33 | GROSELLA-Restaurante | Manuel Pereira | 5ª Ave. Los Palos Grandes | Caracas | 1081 | Venezuela |
| 35 | HILARIÓN-Abastos | Carlos Hernández | Carrera 22 con Ave. Carlos Soublette #8-35 | San Cristóbal | 5022 | Venezuela |
| 46 | LILA-Supermercado | Carlos González | Carrera 52 con Ave. Bolívar #65-98 Llano Largo | Barquisimeto | 3508 | Venezuela |
| 47 | LINO-Delicateses | Felipe Izquierdo | Ave. 5 de Mayo Porlamar | I. de Margarita | 4980 | Venezuela |
| 32 | Great Lakes Food Market | Howard Snyder | 2732 Baker Blvd. | Eugene | 97403 | USA |

(This example only contains the first five, in descending order, by country that would be listed in the Northwind sample database.)

**ORDER BY Multiple Example 1:**

The following SQL statement sorts data from the "Customers" table by "Country" and "CustomerName" columns.

> SELECT * FROM Customers
>
> ORDER BY Country, CustomerName;

Number of Records: 91

| CustomerID | CustomerName | Contact Name | Address | City | PostalCode | Country |
|---|---|---|---|---|---|---|
| 12 | Cactus Comidas para llevar | Patricio Simpson | Cerrito 333 | Buenos Aires | 1010 | Argentina |
| 54 | Océano Atlántico Ltda. | Yvonne Moncada | Ing. Gustavo Moncada 8585 Piso 20-A | Buenos Aires | 1010 | Argentina |
| 64 | Rancho grande | Sergio Gutiérrez | Av. del Libertador 900 | Buenos Aires | 1010 | Argentina |
| 20 | Ernst Handel | Roland Mendel | Kirchgasse 6 | Graz | 8010 | Austria |
| 59 | Piccolo und mehr | Georg Pipps | Geislweg 14 | Salzburg | 5020 | Austria |

(This example only contains the first five ordered by customer name and country that would be listed in the Northwind sample database.)

### ORDER BY Multiple Example 2:

The following SQL statement does the same as above, however, it lists the "Country" column by ascending order and "CustomerName" column by descending order, from the "Customers" table.

*SELECT \* FROM Customers*

*ORDER BY Country ASC, CustomerName DESC;*

Number of Records: 91

| CustomerID | CustomerName | Contact Name | Address | City | PostalCode | Country |
|---|---|---|---|---|---|---|
| 64 | Rancho grande | Sergio Gutiérrez | Av. del Libertador 900 | Buenos Aires | 1010 | Argentina |
| 54 | Océano Atlántico Ltda. | Yvonne Moncada | Ing. Gustavo Moncada 8585 Piso 20-A | Buenos Aires | 1010 | Argentina |
| 12 | Cactus Comidas para llevar | Patricio Simpson | Cerrito 333 | Buenos Aires | 1010 | Argentina |
| 59 | Piccolo und mehr | Georg Pipps | Geislweg 14 | Salzburg | 5020 | Austria |
| 20 | Ernst Handel | Roland Mendel | Kirchgasse 6 | Graz | 8010 | Austria |

# Chapter 9: SQL Insert Into

The SQL INSERT INTO statement can be used to new records into an existing table. This can be done in two methods.

The first method does not specify the exact names of the columns where the data will be inserted, but only specifies values. This is done using the following statement:

> INSERT INTO table_name
>
> VALUES (value1,value2,value3,...);

The second method is more specific. It states both the values as well as the column names for which data will be inserted. This is done using the following statement:

> INSERT INTO table_name (column1,column2,column3,...)
>
> VALUES (value1,value2,value3,...);

| CustomerID | CustomerName | ContactName | Address | City | PostalCode | Country |
|---|---|---|---|---|---|---|
| 87 | Wartian Herkku | Pirkko Koskitalo | Torikatu 38 | Oulu | 90110 | Finland |
| 88 | Wellington Importadora | Paula Parente | Rua do Mercado, 12 | Resende | 08737-363 | Brazil |
| 89 | White Clover Markets | Karl Jablonski | 305 - 14th Ave. S. Suite 3B | Seattle | 98128 | USA |
| 90 | Wilman Kala | Matti Karttunen | Keskuskatu 45 | Helsinki | 21240 | Finland |
| 91 | Wolski | Zbyszek | ul. Filtrowa 68 | Walla | 01-012 | Poland |

**INSERT INTO Example:**

In order to insert a new row into the "Customers" table, you will want to use the following statement:

> INSERT INTO Customers (CustomerName, ContactName, Address, City, PostalCode, Country)

*VALUES ('Cardinal','Tom B. Erichsen','Skagen 21','Stavanger','4006','Norway');*

Below are the changes to the "Customer" table:

| CustomerID | CustomerName | ContactName | Address | City | PostalCode | Country |
|---|---|---|---|---|---|---|
| 87 | Wartian Herkku | Pirkko Koskitalo | Torikatu 38 | Oulu | 90110 | Finland |
| 88 | Wellington Importadora | Paula Parente | Rua do Mercado, 12 | Resende | 08737-363 | Brazil |
| 89 | White Clover Markets | Karl Jablonski | 305 - 14th Ave. S. Suite 3B | Seattle | 98128 | USA |
| 90 | Wilman Kala | Matti Karttunen | Keskuskatu 45 | Helsinki | 21240 | Finland |
| 91 | Wolski | Zbyszek | ul. Filtrowa 68 | Walla | 01-012 | Poland |
| 92 | Cardinal | Tom B. Erichsen | Skagen 21 | Stavanger | 4006 | Norway |

(The CustomerID is automatically updated with a unique value.)

### INSERT INTO Specified Columns Example:

It is possible to add data to specific columns without adding to other columns. For example, to insert data into the "CustomerName", "City", and "Country" columns, use the following statement (remember that the CustomerID column updates automatically):

*INSERT INTO Customers (CustomerName, City, Country)*

*VALUES ('Cardinal', 'Stavanger', 'Norway');*

Below are the changes to the "Customer" table:

| CustomerID | CustomerName | Contact Name | Address | City | PostalCode | Country |
|---|---|---|---|---|---|---|
| 87 | Wartian Herkku | Pirkko Koskitalo | Torikatu 38 | Oulu | 90110 | Finland |
| 88 | Wellington Importadora | Paula Parente | Rua do Mercado, 12 | Resende | 08737-363 | Brazil |
| 89 | White Clover Markets | Karl Jablonski | 305 - 14th Ave. S. Suite 3B | Seattle | 98128 | USA |
| 90 | Wilman Kala | Matti Karttunen | Keskuskatu 45 | Helsinki | 21240 | Finland |
| 91 | Wolski | Zbyszek | ul. Filtrowa 68 | Walla | 01-012 | Poland |
| 92 | Cardinal | null | null | Stavanger | null | Norway |

# Chapter 10: SQL Update

The SQL UPDATE statement is used in order to update the current data contained in a table.

**SQL UPDATE Syntax:**

UPDATE table_name

SET column1=value1,column2=value2,...

WHERE some_column=some_value;

**It is important to keep in mind that the use of the WHERE clause in this statement is very important. Failing to use the WHERE clause to specify which data to update will result in all records being updated.**

**UPDATE Example:**

| CustomerID | CustomerName | Contact Name | Address | City | PostalCode | Country |
|---|---|---|---|---|---|---|
| 1 | Alfreds Futterkiste | Maria Anders | Obere Str. 57 | Berlin | 12209 | Germany |
| 2 | Ana Trujillo Emparedados y helados | Ana Trujillo | Avda. de la Constitución 2222 | México D.F. | 05021 | Mexico |
| 3 | Antonio Moreno Taquería | Antonio Moreno | Mataderos 2312 | México D.F. | 05023 | Mexico |
| 4 | Around the Horn | Thomas Hardy | 120 Hanover Sq. | London | WA1 1DP | UK |
| 5 | Berglunds snabbköp | Christina Berglund | Berguvsvägen 8 | Luleå | S-958 22 | Sweden |

In order to update "Alfreds Futterkiste" win a new "City" and "ContactName" you will use the following statement:

UPDATE Customers

SET ContactName='Alfred Schmidt', City='Hamburg'

WHERE CustomerName='Alfreds Futterkiste';

Below are the changes to the "Customer" table:

| CustomerID | CustomerName | Contact Name | Address | City | PostalCode | Country |
|---|---|---|---|---|---|---|
| 1 | Alfreds Futterkiste | Alfred Schmidt | Obere Str. 57 | Hamburg | 12209 | Germany |
| 2 | Ana Trujillo Emparedados y helados | Ana Trujillo | Avda. de la Constitución 2222 | México D.F. | 05021 | Mexico |
| 3 | Antonio Moreno Taquería | Antonio Moreno | Mataderos 2312 | México D.F. | 05023 | Mexico |
| 4 | Around the Horn | Thomas Hardy | 120 Hanover Sq. | London | WA1 1DP | UK |
| 5 | Berglunds snabbköp | Christina Berglund | Berguvsvägen 8 | Luleå | S-958 22 | Sweden |

**UPDATE While Omitting WHERE Clause Example:**

As previously stated, omitting the where clause will result in all information being updated. An example of what not to do would be using a statement like this:

> *UPDATE Customers*
>
> *SET ContactName='Alfred Schmidt', City='Hamburg';*

Below are the changes to the "Customer" table:

| CustomerID | CustomerName | ContactName | Address | City | PostalCode | Country |
|---|---|---|---|---|---|---|
| 1 | Alfreds Futterkiste | Alfred Schmidt | Obere Str. 57 | Hamburg | 12209 | Germany |
| 2 | Ana Trujillo Emparedados y helados | Alfred Schmidt | Avda. de la Constitución 2222 | Hamburg | 05021 | Mexico |
| 3 | Antonio Moreno Taquería | Alfred Schmidt | Mataderos 2312 | Hamburg | 05023 | Mexico |
| 4 | Around the Horn | Alfred Schmidt | 120 Hanover Sq. | Hamburg | WA1 1DP | UK |
| 5 | Berglunds snabbköp | Alfred Schmidt | Berguvsvägen 8 | Hamburg | S-958 22 | Sweden |

As you can see, every ContactName has now been updated to Alfred Schmidt. You should try to avoid this and always include the WHERE clause.

# Chapter 11: SQL Delete

The DELETE SQL statement is used in order to delete rows from an existing table.

**SQL DELETE Syntax:**

> DELETE FROM table_name
>
> WHERE some_column=some_value;

**Similar to the UPDATE statement, failure to use the WHERE clause in DELETE statement can result in all records being deleted. Double check and ensure proper usage of the WHERE clause.**

**DELETE Example:**

| CustomerID | CustomerName | Contact Name | Address | City | PostalCode | Country |
|---|---|---|---|---|---|---|
| 1 | Alfreds Futterkiste | Maria Anders | Obere Str. 57 | Berlin | 12209 | Germany |
| 2 | Ana Trujillo Emparedados y helados | Ana Trujillo | Avda. de la Constitución 2222 | México D.F. | 05021 | Mexico |
| 3 | Antonio Moreno Taquería | Antonio Moreno | Mataderos 2312 | México D.F. | 05023 | Mexico |
| 4 | Around the Horn | Thomas Hardy | 120 Hanover Sq. | London | WA1 1DP | UK |
| 5 | Berglunds snabbköp | Christina Berglund | Berguvsväg en 8 | Luleå | S-958 22 | Sweden |

In order to remove or delete "Alfreds Futterkiste" from "Customers" table, you will need to use the following statement:

> DELETE FROM Customers
>
> WHERE CustomerName='Alfreds Futterkiste' AND ContactName='Maria Anders';

Below are the changes to the "Customer" table:

| CustomerID | CustomerName | Contact Name | Address | City | PostalCode | Country |
|---|---|---|---|---|---|---|
| 2 | Ana Trujillo Emparedados y helados | Ana Trujillo | Avda. de la Constitución 2222 | México D.F. | 05021 | Mexico |
| 3 | Antonio Moreno Taquería | Antonio Moreno | Mataderos 2312 | México D.F. | 05023 | Mexico |
| 4 | Around the Horn | Thomas Hardy | 120 Hanover Sq. | London | WA1 1DP | UK |
| 5 | Berglunds snabbköp | Christina Berglund | Berguvsväg en 8 | Luleå | S-958 22 | Sweden |

**DELETE All Data Example:**

If you wish to delete all of the data contained in a table, without deleting the table itself, you can omit the WHERE clause. The benefit of this is that the table maintains its structure, indexes, and attributes. You can do this using the following statement:

> *DELETE FROM table_name;*

or

> *DELETE * FROM table_name;*

**DELETING RECORDS CAN NOT BE UNDONE. It is very important to double check your statement to ensure usage of the WHERE clause unless you are wanting to delete all data in the table.**

# Chapter 12: SQL Injection

Take special care when using an SQL Injection, as it can destroy your database.

So far you have learned how to use SQL to retrieve, update, and delete database data. When used to display data on a webpage, it is normal to let users input their search values. It is easy to change SQL statements to provide users with selected data by using SQL and a piece of computer code:

**Server Code Example:**

> *txtUserId = getRequestString("UserId");*
>
> *txtSQL = "SELECT * FROM Users WHERE UserId = " + txtUserId;*

In this example, a select statement is created by adding txtUserId, which is a variable, to a select string. The variable is fetched from the request, or user input, to the page.

The remainder of this chapter concerns the dangers of using user input on SQL statements.

**SQL Injection:**

Malicious individuals may use this technique via a web page input in order to inject SQL commands into an SQL statement. This can alter the statement and compromise the web application's security.

1=1 is always true.

Go back to the previous example of the server code. If the purpose is to create an SQL statement that selects a user with a given user ID, then there is nothing to prevent someone from entering an incorrect input, instead entering something "smart" and using something like this:

> UserId: *105 or 1=1*

Server Result

> *SELECT * FROM Users WHERE UserId = 105 or 1=1*

This is a valid SQL, and this will return all data from the table labeled "Users" since WHERE 1=1 is always true. This may not seem like a large concern, but what if the table contains secure information, such as social security numbers, or usernames and passwords?

Another similar example is:

> SELECT UserId, Name, Password FROM Users WHERE UserId = 105 or 1=1

By simply inserting "105 or 1=1" into the input box, a smart hacker can potentially gain all usernames and passwords from a database.

**SQL Injection Based on ""="" is Always True**

The following is commonly used in order to verify a user's login to a website:

User Name:

Password:

Server Code

uName = *getRequestString("UserName");*

uPass = *getRequestString("UserPass");*

sql = *"SELECT * FROM Users WHERE Name ='" + uName + "' AND Pass ='" + uPass + ""*

For this, a smart hacker can potentially gain access to usernames and passwords by enter "or""=" into the username or password text field. This will cause the server to create a valid statement:

> SELECT * FROM Users WHERE Name ="" or ""="" AND Pass ="" or ""=""

This SQL is valid as well. It will return all data from the "Users" table, since WHERE ""="" is always true.

**Injection Based on Batched Statements Example:**

Batched statements, when separated by a semicolon, is supported by most databases.

> SELECT * FROM Users; DROP TABLE Suppliers

This SQL will, again, return all rows in the Users table. Then, however, it will delete the "Suppliers" table.

Using the following server code:

> txtUserId = *getRequestString("UserId");*
>
> txtSQL = *"SELECT * FROM Users WHERE UserId = " + txtUserId;*

And this input:

User id: *105; DROP TABLE Suppliers*

Would result in a valid SQL Statement:

*SELECT \* FROM Users WHERE UserId = 105; DROP TABLE Suppliers*

**Protection Parameters**

The use of blacklist of words or characters to search for an SQL input is used by some web developers in order to prevent SQL injection attacks. This is not recommended. The reason is that specific words and characters, such as delete, drop, quotation marks and semicolons are commonly used in everyday language and should be allowed. The only proven way to protect from SQL injection attacks is the proper use of SQL parameters, which are values added in a controlled manner to an SQL query at the time of execution.

**ASP.NET Razor Example**

*txtUserId = getRequestString("UserId");*

*txtSQL = "SELECT \* FROM Users WHERE UserId = @0";*

*db.Execute(txtSQL,txtUserId);*

Please note that the @ symbol represents the parameters in the SQL statement. The engine checks these parameters to ensure it is correct for the column and they are treated literally, and separate from the SQL that is being executed.

**One More Example:**

*txtNam = getRequestString("CustomerName");*

*txtAdd = getRequestString("Address");*

*txtCit = getRequestString("City");*

*txtSQL = "INSERT INTO Customers (CustomerName,Address,City)*

*Values(@0,@1,@2)";*

*db.Execute(txtSQL,txtNam,txtAdd,txtCit);*

SQL Injection can be a website's most exploitable weakness, so learning to avoid this is paramount.

## More Examples:

Here are some examples that will show you how parameterized queries are built in frequently used web languages:

SELECT STATEMENT IN ASP.NET:

> *txtUserId = getRequestString("UserId");*
>
> *sql = "SELECT * FROM Customers WHERE CustomerId = @0";*
>
> *command = new SqlCommand(sql);*
>
> *command.Parameters.AddWithValue("@0",txtUserID);*
>
> *command.ExecuteReader();*

INSERT INTO STATEMENT IN ASP.NET:

> *txtNam = getRequestString("CustomerName");*
>
> *txtAdd = getRequestString("Address");*
>
> *txtCit = getRequestString("City");*
>
> *txtSQL = "INSERT INTO Customers (CustomerName,Address,City)*

*Values(@0,@1,@2)";*

> *command = new SqlCommand(txtSQL);*
>
> *command.Parameters.AddWithValue("@0",txtNam);*
>
> *command.Parameters.AddWithValue("@1",txtAdd);*
>
> *command.Parameters.AddWithValue("@2",txtCit);*
>
> *command.ExecuteNonQuery();*

INSERT INTO STATEMENT IN PHP:

> *$stmt = $dbh->prepare("INSERT INTO Customers (CustomerName,Address,City)*

*VALUES (:nam, :add, :cit)");*

> *$stmt->bindParam(':nam', $txtNam);*
>
> *$stmt->bindParam(':add', $txtAdd);*
>
> *$stmt->bindParam(':cit', $txtCit);*
>
> *$stmt->execute();*

# Chapter 13: SQL Select Top

The SQL SELECT TOP clause is used in order to specify the number of records that will be returned, which is very useful on tables containing thousands of records. It is important to note that not all databases support this clause.

**MS Access Syntax / SQL Server Syntax:**

*SELECT TOP number|percent column_name(s)*

*FROM table_name;*

**SELECT TOP Equivalent in Oracle and MySQL:**

**Oracle Syntax:**

*SELECT column_name(s)*

*FROM table_name*

*WHERE ROWNUM <= number;*

Example:

*SELECT ***

*FROM Persons*

*WHERE ROWNUM <=5;*

**MySQL Syntax:**

*SELECT column_name(s)*

*FROM table_name*

*LIMIT number;*

Example:

*SELECT ***

*FROM Persons*

*LIMIT 5;*

**SELECT TOP Example:**

| CustomerID | CustomerName | Contact Name | Address | City | PostalCode | Country |
|---|---|---|---|---|---|---|
| 1 | Alfreds Futterkiste | Maria Anders | Obere Str. 57 | Berlin | 12209 | Germany |
| 2 | Ana Trujillo Emparedados y helados | Ana Trujillo | Avda. de la Constitució n 2222 | México D.F. | 05021 | Mexico |
| 3 | Antonio Moreno Taquería | Antonio Moreno | Mataderos 2312 | México D.F. | 05023 | Mexico |
| 4 | Around the Horn | Thomas Hardy | 120 Hanover Sq. | London | WA1 1DP | UK |
| 5 | Berglunds snabbköp | Christina Berglund | Berguvsväg en 8 | Luleå | S-958 22 | Sweden |

In order to select the first two rows of the "Customers" table, you would use the following:

    *SELECT TOP 2 \* FROM Customers;*

Number of Records: 2

| CustomerID | CustomerName | ContactName | Address | City | PostalCode | Country |
|---|---|---|---|---|---|---|
| 1 | Alfreds Futterkiste | Maria Anders | Obere Str. 57 | Berlin | 12209 | Germany |
| 2 | Ana Trujillo Emparedados y helados | Ana Trujillo | Avda. de la Constitución 2222 | México D.F. | 05021 | Mexico |

**SELECT TOP Percentage Example:**

The next statement will return the first 50% of the "Customers" table records:

    *SELECT TOP 50 PERCENT \* FROM Customers;*

# Chapter 14: SQL Like

The SQL Like operator can be used within a WHERE clause in order to search for a pattern in a column.

**SQL LIKE Syntax**

> SELECT column_name(s)
>
> FROM table_name
>
> WHERE column_name LIKE pattern;

**LIKE Example:**

| CustomerID | CustomerName | ContactName | Address | City | PostalCode | Country |
|---|---|---|---|---|---|---|
| 1 | Alfreds Futterkiste | Maria Anders | Obere Str. 57 | Berlin | 12209 | Germany |
| 2 | Ana Trujillo Emparedados y helados | Ana Trujillo | Avda. de la Constitución 2222 | México D.F. | 05021 | Mexico |
| 3 | Antonio Moreno Taquería | Antonio Moreno | Mataderos 2312 | México D.F. | 05023 | Mexico |
| 4 | Around the Horn | Thomas Hardy | 120 Hanover Sq. | London | WA1 1DP | UK |
| 5 | Berglunds snabbköp | Christina Berglund | Berguvsvägen 8 | Luleå | S-958 22 | Sweden |

In order to select all customers with a "City" starting with the letter "s" you will use the following statement:

> SELECT * FROM Customers
>
> WHERE City LIKE 's%';

Number of Records: 12

| CustomerID | CustomerName | Contact Name | Address | City | PostalCode | Country |
|---|---|---|---|---|---|---|
| 7 | Blondel père et fils | Frédérique Citeaux | 24, place Kléber | Strasbourg | 67000 | France |
| 15 | Comércio Mineiro | Pedro Afonso | Av. dos Lusíadas, 23 | São Paulo | 05432-043 | Brazil |
| 21 | Familia Arquibaldo | Aria Cruz | Rua Orós, 92 | São Paulo | 05442-030 | Brazil |
| 30 | Godos Cocina Típica | José Pedro Freyre | C/ Romero, 33 | Sevilla | 41101 | Spain |
| 35 | HILARION-Abastos | Carlos Hernández | Carrera 22 con Ave. Carlos Soublette #8-35 | San Cristóbal | 5022 | Venezuela |
| 45 | Let's Stop N Shop | Jaime Yorres | 87 Polk St. Suite 5 | San Francisco | 94117 | USA |
| 59 | Piccolo und mehr | Georg Pipps | Geislweg 14 | Salzburg | 5020 | Austria |
| 62 | Queen Cozinha | Lúcia Carvalho | Alameda dos Canários, 891 | São Paulo | 05487-020 | Brazil |
| 70 | Santé Gourmet | Jonas Bergulfsen | Erling Skakkes gate 78 | Stavern | 4110 | Norway |
| 81 | Tradição Hipermercados | Anabela Domingues | Av. Inês de Castro, 414 | São Paulo | 05634-030 | Brazil |
| 86 | Die Wandernde Kuh | Rita Müller | Adenauerallee 900 | Stuttgart | 70563 | Germany |
| 89 | White Clover Markets | Karl Jablonski | 305 - 14th Ave. S. Suite 3B | Seattle | 98128 | USA |

The "%" sign is used in order to define missing letters or wildcards before and after the pattern. Wildcards will be discussed in the next chapter.

Alternately, you can find all the customers with a "City" ending with the letter "s" using the following statement"

    *SELECT \* FROM Customers*

*WHERE City LIKE '%s';*

Or you can select all customers in a "Country" with "land" in the name, with this statement:

*SELECT * FROM Customers*

*WHERE Country LIKE '%land%';*

The use of the keyword "NOT" will allow you to select records outside of that pattern, for example, if you wanted to select all customers with a "Country" that does not contain "land" then you could use the following statement:

*SELECT * FROM Customers*

*WHERE Country NOT LIKE '%land%';*

# Chapter 15: SQL Wildcards

A wildcard character can be used with the LIKE operator in order to search for data within the table, using the wildcard as a substitute for other characters.

Here is a list of SQL wildcards:

| Wildcard | Description |
| --- | --- |
| % | A substitute for zero or more characters |
| _ | A substitute for a single character |
| [charlist] | Sets and ranges of characters to match |
| [^charlist] or [!charlist] | Matches only a character NOT specified within the brackets |

## SQL Wildcard Examples:

| CustomerID | CustomerName | ContactName | Address | City | PostalCode | Country |
| --- | --- | --- | --- | --- | --- | --- |
| 1 | Alfreds Futterkiste | Maria Anders | Obere Str. 57 | Berlin | 12209 | Germany |
| 2 | Ana Trujillo Emparedados y helados | Ana Trujillo | Avda. de la Constitución 2222 | México D.F. | 05021 | Mexico |
| 3 | Antonio Moreno Taquería | Antonio Moreno | Mataderos 2312 | México D.F. | 05023 | Mexico |
| 4 | Around the Horn | Thomas Hardy | 120 Hanover Sq. | London | WA1 1DP | UK |
| 5 | Berglunds snabbköp | Christina Berglund | Berguvsväg en 8 | Luleå | S-958 22 | Sweden |

## % Wildcard Example:

In order to select all customers with a "City" that starts with "ber" use the following statement:

> SELECT * FROM Customers
> 
> WHERE City LIKE 'ber%';

Number of Records: 3

| CustomerID | CustomerName | Contact Name | Address | City | PostalCode | Country |
|---|---|---|---|---|---|---|
| 1 | Alfreds Futterkiste | Maria Anders | Obere Str. 57 | Berlin | 12209 | Germany |
| 14 | Chop-suey Chinese | Yang Wang | Hauptstr. 29 | Bern | 3012 | Switzerland |
| 49 | Magazzini Alimentari Riuniti | Giovanni Rovelli | Via Ludovico il Moro 22 | Bergamo | 24100 | Italy |

In order to select all customers with a "City" containing "es" use the following statement:

SELECT * FROM Customers

WHERE City LIKE '%es%';

This will return results for every customer with a city containing "es" anywhere in the "City" Column.

In order to select all customers with a "City" containing "erlin" use the following statement:

SELECT * FROM Customers

WHERE City LIKE '_erlin';

You can make this as complex as necessary. For example, you can obtain results for every customer in a "City" with starting character "L" and then any character, then followed by "n", then followed by any other character, and finally followed by "on" using a statement similar to this:

SELECT * FROM Customers

WHERE City LIKE 'L_n_on';

Number of Records: 6

| CustomerID | CustomerName | Contact Name | Address | City | PostalCode | Country |
|---|---|---|---|---|---|---|
| 4 | Around the Horn | Thomas Hardy | 120 Hanover Sq. | London | WA1 1DP | UK |
| 11 | B's Beverages | Victoria Ashworth | Fauntleroy Circus | London | EC2 5NT | UK |
| 16 | Consolidated Holdings | Elizabeth Brown | Berkeley Gardens 12 Brewery | London | WX1 6LT | UK |
| 19 | Eastern Connection | Ann Devon | 35 King George | London | WX3 6FW | UK |
| 53 | North/South | Simon Crowther | South House 300 Queensbridge | London | SW7 1RZ | UK |
| 72 | Seven Seas Imports | Hari Kumar | 90 Wadhurst Rd. | London | OX15 4NB | UK |

**Charlist Wildcard Example:**

In order to have data returned for all customers in a "City" with "b", "s", or "p", use the following statement:

> SELECT * FROM Customers
>
> WHERE City LIKE '[bsp]%';

In order to have data returned on all customers with a "City" starting with "a", "b", or "c" use this:

> SELECT * FROM Customers
>
> WHERE City LIKE '[a-c]%';

Again, you can do the opposite, and return data on all customers with a "City" not containing "b", "s", or "p" using the following statement:

> SELECT * FROM Customers
>
> WHERE City LIKE '[!bsp]%';

or

> SELECT * FROM Customers
>
> WHERE City NOT LIKE '[bsp]%';

# Chapter 16: SQL In

The SQL IN operator allows specification of other values within the WHERE clause.

**SQL IN Syntax:**

> SELECT column_name(s)
> 
> FROM table_name
> 
> WHERE column_name IN (value1,value2,...);

**IN Operator Example:**

| Customer ID | CustomerName | ContactName | Address | City | PostalCode | Country |
|---|---|---|---|---|---|---|
| 1 | Alfreds Futterkiste | Maria Anders | Obere Str. 57 | Berlin | 12209 | Germany |
| 2 | Ana Trujillo Emparedados y helados | Ana Trujillo | Avda. de la Constitución 2222 | México D.F. | 05021 | Mexico |
| 3 | Antonio Moreno Taquería | Antonio Moreno | Mataderos 2312 | México D.F. | 05023 | Mexico |
| 4 | Around the Horn | Thomas Hardy | 120 Hanover Sq. | London | WA1 1DP | UK |
| 5 | Berglunds snabbköp | Christina Berglund | Berguvsvägen 8 | Luleå | S-958 22 | Sweden |

In order to return all data from customers in the "City" of "Paris" or "London" use this statement:

> SELECT * FROM Customers
> 
> WHERE City IN ('Paris','London');

Number of Records: 8

| CustomerID | CustomerName | Contact Name | Address | City | PostalCode | Country |
|---|---|---|---|---|---|---|
| 4 | Around the Horn | Thomas Hardy | 120 Hanover Sq. | London | WA1 1DP | UK |
| 11 | B's Beverages | Victoria Ashworth | Fauntleroy Circus | London | EC2 5NT | UK |
| 16 | Consolidated Holdings | Elizabeth Brown | Berkeley Gardens 12 Brewery | London | WX1 6LT | UK |
| 19 | Eastern Connection | Ann Devon | 35 King George | London | WX3 6FW | UK |
| 53 | North/South | Simon Crowther | South House 300 Queensbridge | London | SW7 1RZ | UK |
| 57 | Paris spécialités | Marie Bertrand | 265, boulevard Charonne | Paris | 75012 | France |
| 72 | Seven Seas Imports | Hari Kumar | 90 Wadhurst Rd. | London | OX15 4NB | UK |
| 74 | Spécialités du monde | Dominique Perrier | 25, rue Lauriston | Paris | 75016 | France |

# Chapter 17: SQL Between

The BETWEEN operator is used in order to select values within a specified range, containing numbers, dates, or text.

**SQL BETWEEN Syntax:**

SELECT column_name(s)

FROM table_name

WHERE column_name BETWEEN value1 AND value2;

**BETWEEN Operator Example:**

Below is a selection from the Northwind sample database, this is the "Products" table.

| ProductID | ProductName | SupplierID | CategoryID | Unit | Price |
|---|---|---|---|---|---|
| 1 | Chais | 1 | 1 | 10 boxes x 20 bags | 18 |
| 2 | Chang | 1 | 1 | 24 - 12 oz bottles | 19 |
| 3 | Aniseed Syrup | 1 | 2 | 12 - 550 ml bottles | 10 |
| 4 | Chef Anton's Cajun Seasoning | 1 | 2 | 48 - 6 oz jars | 22 |
| 5 | Chef Anton's Gumbo Mix | 1 | 2 | 36 boxes | 21.35 |

In order to return all product data with a price between 10 and 20, use the following statement:

SELECT * FROM Products

WHERE Price BETWEEN 10 AND 20;

Again, you can do the opposite, using NOT. In order to return all product data outside of the previously specified range, use the following statement:

SELECT * FROM Products

WHERE Price NOT BETWEEN 10 AND 20;

You can also utilize the IN along with the BETWEEN operator in order to return all product data with a price between 10 and 20, and also state that the products with a "CatagorID" of 1, 2, or 3 should not be returned. You can do so using the following statement:

SELECT * FROM Products

WHERE (Price BETWEEN 10 AND 20)

AND NOT CategoryID IN (1,2,3);

In order to use the text value BETWEEN operator to return all product data with a ProductName with any letter between 'c' and 'm' using the following statement:

SELECT * FROM Products

WHERE ProductName BETWEEN 'C' AND 'M';

Much like before, you can do the opposite and return all product data with a ProductName with any letter that is not between 'c' and 'm' by using the following statement:

SELECT * FROM Products

WHERE ProductName NOT BETWEEN 'C' AND 'M';

Below is the "Orders" table:

| ProductID | ProductName | SupplierID | CategoryID | Unit | Price |
|---|---|---|---|---|---|
| 1 | Chais | 1 | 1 | 10 boxes x 20 bags | 18 |
| 2 | Chang | 1 | 1 | 24 - 12 oz bottles | 19 |
| 3 | Aniseed Syrup | 1 | 2 | 12 - 550 ml bottles | 10 |
| 4 | Chef Anton's Cajun Seasoning | 1 | 2 | 48 - 6 oz jars | 22 |
| 5 | Chef Anton's Gumbo Mix | 1 | 2 | 36 boxes | 21.35 |

In order to return all order data with an order date between '04-July-1996' and '09-July-1996' you will use the following statement:

> SELECT * FROM Orders
>
> WHERE OrderDate BETWEEN #07/04/1996# AND #07/09/1996#;

It is important to note that different results can be achieved with different databases when using the BETWEEN operator. Some databases use the BETWEEN operator to select fields and include test values, whereas others exclude the test values. Others will do the same but only include the first test value and not the last test value. It would be best to check to see which way your database reacts.

# Chapter 18: SQL Aliases

SQL Aliases are used in order to temporarily change the names of database tables or column headings. This is done in order to make them more readable.

**SQL Columns Alias Syntax:**

    SELECT column_name AS alias_name

    FROM table_name;

**SQL Tables Alias Syntax:**

    SELECT column_name(s)

    FROM table_name AS alias_name;

**ALIAS Example:**

Below is a portion of the "Customers" table:

| ProductID | ProductName | SupplierID | CategoryID | Unit | Price |
|---|---|---|---|---|---|
| 1 | Chais | 1 | 1 | 10 boxes x 20 bags | 18 |
| 2 | Chang | 1 | 1 | 24 - 12 oz bottles | 19 |
| 3 | Aniseed Syrup | 1 | 2 | 12 - 550 ml bottles | 10 |
| 4 | Chef Anton's Cajun Seasoning | 1 | 2 | 48 - 6 oz jars | 22 |
| 5 | Chef Anton's Gumbo Mix | 1 | 2 | 36 boxes | 21.35 |

Below is a portion of the "Orders" table:

| OrderID | CustomerID | EmployeeID | OrderDate | ShipperID |
|---------|------------|------------|------------|-----------|
| 10354 | 58 | 8 | 1996-11-14 | 3 |
| 10355 | 4 | 6 | 1996-11-15 | 1 |
| 10356 | 86 | 6 | 1996-11-18 | 2 |

**Columns Alias:**

The following statement has two aliases, one for the ContactName column and another for the CustomerName column. Double quotations or square brackets are required if the column name has spaces in it:

> SELECT CustomerName AS Customer, ContactName AS [Contact Person]
>
> FROM Customers;

When the return-set is viewed, you will then see that "ContactName" has been replaced with "Contact Person" and "CustomerName" has been replaced with "Customer".

A great use for this is to use a statement to combine all aspects of the address, including the Address, the City, the PostalCode, and the Country. You can do so using the alias named "Address" with the following statement:

> SELECT CustomerName, Address+', '+City+', '+PostalCode+', '+Country AS Address
>
> FROM Customers;

In order to do the same thing in MySQL, use the following statement:

> SELECT CustomerName, CONCAT(Address,', ',City,', ',PostalCode,', ',Country) AS Address
>
> FROM Customers;

**Tables Alias:**

This statement is used to select all orders from the customer with the CustomerID=4 (Around the Horn). We are using the "Customers" and "Orders" tables above, and we give the tables the aliases of "c" and "o" respectively.

SELECT o.OrderID, o.OrderDate, c.CustomerName

FROM Customers AS c, Orders AS o

WHERE c.CustomerName="Around the Horn" AND c.CustomerID=o.CustomerID;

Number of Records: 2

| OrderID | OrderDate | CustomerName |
|---|---|---|
| 10355 | 1996-11-15 | Around the Horn |
| 10383 | 1996-12-16 | Around the Horn |

Here is the same statement without aliases:

SELECT Orders.OrderID, Orders.OrderDate, Customers.CustomerName

FROM Customers, Orders

WHERE Customers.CustomerName="Around the Horn" AND Customers.CustomerID=Orders.CustomerID;

This provides the same result.

**When to Use Aliases:**

- One or more table being queried.
- The query uses functions
- Column names are illegible or large
- When combining two or more columns

# Chapter 19: SQL Joins

Joins are used in order to combine rows from multiple tables, based upon a commonality between the two. The most common of which is the INNER Join, also known as the simple join.

First, look at this selection from the "Orders" table:

| OrderID | CustomerID | OrderDate |
|---|---|---|
| 10308 | 2 | 1996-09-18 |
| 10309 | 37 | 1996-09-19 |
| 10310 | 77 | 1996-09-20 |

Then look at this selection from the "Customers" table:

| CustomerID | CustomerName | ContactName | Country |
|---|---|---|---|
| 1 | Alfreds Futterkiste | Maria Anders | Germany |
| 2 | Ana Trujillo Emparedados y helados | Ana Trujillo | Mexico |
| 3 | Antonio Moreno Taqueria | Antonio Moreno | Mexico |

The "CustomerID" column in the "Orders" table is directly related to the "CustomerID" in the "Customers" table.

Now, by running the following statement containing an inner join:

> SELECT Orders.OrderID, Customers.CustomerName, Orders.OrderDate
>
> FROM Orders
>
> INNER JOIN Customers
>
> ON Orders.CustomerID=Customers.CustomerID;

We will end up with this:

| OrderID | CustomerName | OrderDate |
|---|---|---|
| 10308 | Ana Trujillo Emparedados y helados | 9/18/1996 |
| 10365 | Antonio Moreno Taqueria | 11/27/1996 |
| 10383 | Around the Horn | 12/16/1996 |
| 10355 | Around the Horn | 11/15/1996 |
| 10278 | Berglunds snabbköp | 8/12/1996 |

**Different Variations of SQL JOINs:**

- INNER JOIN: returns all rows containing at least one match in each table.
- Left JOIN: returns all rows from left table and the matched rows from the table on the right.
- RIGHT JOIN: returns all rows from the right table and the matched rows from the left table
- FULL JOIN: returns all rows when if there is a match in one table.

# Chapter 20: SQL Inner Join

The INNER JOIN keyword will, as long as there is a match between columns on both tables, will select all rows from both tables.

**INNER JOIN Syntax:**

*SELECT column_name(s)*

*FROM table1*

*INNER JOIN table2*

*ON table1.column_name=table2.column_name;*

or:

*SELECT column_name(s)*

*FROM table1*

*JOIN table2*

*ON table1.column_name=table2.column_name;*

**Keep in mind, INNER JOIN = JOIN**

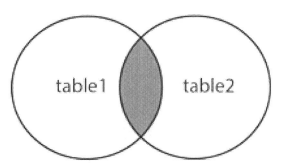

**INNER JOIN Example:**

"Customers" table:

| CustomerID | CustomerName | Contact Name | Address | City | PostalCode | Country |
|---|---|---|---|---|---|---|
| 1 | Alfreds Futterkiste | Maria Anders | Obere Str. 57 | Berlin | 12209 | Germany |
| 2 | Ana Trujillo Emparedados y helados | Ana Trujillo | Avda. de la Constitució n 2222 | México D.F. | 05021 | Mexico |
| 3 | Antonio Moreno Taqueria | Antonio Moreno | Mataderos 2312 | México D.F. | 05023 | Mexico |

"Orders" table"

| OrderID | CustomerID | EmployeeID | OrderDate | ShipperID |
|---|---|---|---|---|
| 10308 | 2 | 7 | 1996-09-18 | 3 |
| 10309 | 37 | 3 | 1996-09-19 | 1 |
| 10310 | 77 | 8 | 1996-09-20 | 2 |

In order to return all data on customers with orders, use the following statement:

*SELECT Customers.CustomerName, Orders.OrderID*

*FROM Customers*

*INNER JOIN Orders*

*ON Customers.CustomerID=Orders.CustomerID*

*ORDER BY Customers.CustomerName;*

Doing this will return the customer name along with the order number. If the "Customers" table has rows that do not have matches in "Orders", that data will not be returned.

# Chapter 21: SQL Left Join

The LEFT JOIN keyword will return all rows from table1, or the left table, and matching rows from table2, the right table. You will return NULL in the right side when there is no match.

**SQL LEFT JOIN Syntax:**

*SELECT column_name(s)*

*FROM table1*

*LEFT JOIN table2*

*ON table1.column_name=table2.column_name;*

or:

*SELECT column_name(s)*

*FROM table1*

*LEFT OUTER JOIN table2*

*ON table1.column_name=table2.column_name;*

Please note that LEFT JOIN is referred to as LEFT OUTER JOIN in some databases.

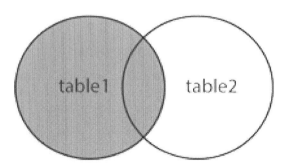

LEFT JOIN

**LEFT JOIN Example:**

"Customers" table:

| CustomerID | CustomerName | Contact Name | Address | City | PostalCode | Country |
|---|---|---|---|---|---|---|
| 1 | Alfreds Futterkiste | Maria Anders | Obere Str. 57 | Berlin | 12209 | Germany |
| 2 | Ana Trujillo Emparedados y helados | Ana Trujillo | Avda. de la Constitución 2222 | México D.F. | 05021 | Mexico |
| 3 | Antonio Moreno Taquería | Antonio Moreno | Mataderos 2312 | México D.F. | 05023 | Mexico |

"Orders" table:

| OrderID | CustomerID | EmployeeID | OrderDate | ShipperID |
|---|---|---|---|---|
| 10308 | 2 | 7 | 1996-09-18 | 3 |
| 10309 | 37 | 3 | 1996-09-19 | 1 |
| 10310 | 77 | 8 | 1996-09-20 | 2 |

In order to return data on all customers and order data that they may have, use the following statement:

*SELECT Customers.CustomerName, Orders.OrderID*

*FROM Customers*

*LEFT JOIN Orders*

*ON Customers.CustomerID=Orders.CustomerID*

*ORDER BY Customers.CustomerName;*

In this instance, all rows of customers will be returned along with order data or order numbers, and if there is no order data, you will see NULL instead of an order number.

# Chapter 22: SQL Right Join

The SQL RIGHT JOIN keyword does the opposite of LEFT JOIN, whereas it returns all rows from table 2, or the right table, with matching rows from table 2, or the left table. NULL will populate on the left side with no match.

**SQL RIGHT JOIN Syntax:**

*SELECT column_name(s)*

*FROM table1*

*RIGHT JOIN table2*

*ON table1.column_name=table2.column_name;*

or:

*SELECT column_name(s)*

*FROM table1*

*RIGHT OUTER JOIN table2*

*ON table1.column_name=table2.column_name;*

Please note that LEFT JOIN is referred to as LEFT OUTER JOIN in some databases.

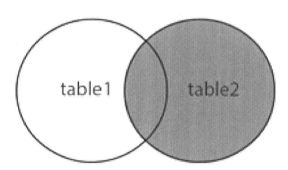

**RIGHT JOIN Example:**

"Orders" table:

| OrderID | CustomerID | EmployeeID | OrderDate | ShipperID |
|---|---|---|---|---|
| 10308 | 2 | 7 | 1996-09-18 | 3 |
| 10309 | 37 | 3 | 1996-09-19 | 1 |
| 10310 | 77 | 8 | 1996-09-20 | 2 |

"Employees" table:

| EmployeeID | LastName | FirstName | BirthDate | Photo | Notes |
|---|---|---|---|---|---|
| 1 | Davolio | Nancy | 12/8/1968 | EmpID1.pic | Education includes a BA in psychology..... |
| 2 | Fuller | Andrew | 2/19/1952 | EmpID2.pic | Andrew received his BTS commercial and.... |
| 3 | Leverling | Janet | 8/30/1963 | EmpID3.pic | Janet has a BS degree in chemistry.... |

In order to return data on all employees along with any order date that has been placed, use the following statement:

SELECT Orders.OrderID, Employees.FirstName

FROM Orders

RIGHT JOIN Employees

ON Orders.EmployeeID=Employees.EmployeeID

ORDER BY Orders.OrderID;

In this instance, the order numbers are returned left, and the employee FirstName is listed on the right. In cases where there is no order data, the left will show NULL.

# Chapter 23: SQL Full Join

The SQL FULL OUTER JOIN keyword will return all rows from table1, left, and from table2, right, regardless of matching data.

**SQL FULL OUTER JOIN Syntax:**

*SELECT column_name(s)*

*FROM table1*

*FULL OUTER JOIN table2*

*ON table1.column_name=table2.column_name;*

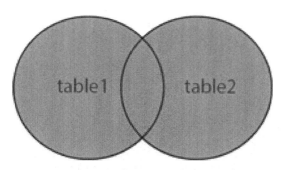

**FULL OUTER JOIN Example:**

"Customer" table:

| CustomerID | CustomerName | Contact Name | Address | City | PostalCode | Country |
|---|---|---|---|---|---|---|
| 1 | Alfreds Futterkiste | Maria Anders | Obere Str. 57 | Berlin | 12209 | Germany |
| 2 | Ana Trujillo Emparedados y helados | Ana Trujillo | Avda. de la Constitución 2222 | México D.F. | 05021 | Mexico |
| 3 | Antonio Moreno Taquería | Antonio Moreno | Mataderos 2312 | México D.F. | 05023 | Mexico |

"Orders" table:

| OrderID | CustomerID | EmployeeID | OrderDate | ShipperID |
|---------|------------|------------|------------|-----------|
| 10308 | 2 | 7 | 1996-09-18 | 3 |
| 10309 | 37 | 3 | 1996-09-19 | 1 |
| 10310 | 77 | 8 | 1996-09-20 | 2 |

In order to return all customers and all orders, use the following statement:

>SELECT Customers.CustomerName, Orders.OrderID
>
>FROM Customers
>
>FULL OUTER JOIN Orders
>
>ON Customers.CustomerID=Orders.CustomerID
>
>ORDER BY Customers.CustomerName;

Doing so may result in data returned like this:

| CustomerName | OrderID |
|--------------|---------|
| Alfreds Futterkiste | |
| Ana Trujillo Emparedados y helados | 10308 |
| Antonio Moreno Taqueria | 10365 |
| | 10382 |
| | 10351 |

The FULL OUTER keyword will return all rows from both tables, as well as any rows that do not have matches.

# Chapter 24: SQL Union

The SQL UNION operator is used to combine the results of multiple statements. Each SELECT statement within a UNION have to have an equal number of columns, with similar data types, and the statements must be in the same order.

**SQL UNION Syntax:**

> SELECT column_name(s) FROM table1
>
> UNION
>
> SELECT column_name(s) FROM table2;

By default, the UNION operator will only select distinct values. In order to return duplicate values, use the ALL keyword within the UNION.

**SQL UNION ALL Syntax:**

> SELECT column_name(s) FROM table1
>
> UNION ALL
>
> SELECT column_name(s) FROM table2;

In the result-set of the UNION, the column names are usually equal to the column names in the first SELECT statement.

**UNION Example:**

"Customer" table:

| CustomerID | CustomerName | ContactName | Address | City | PostalCode | Country |
|---|---|---|---|---|---|---|
| 1 | Alfreds Futterkiste | Maria Anders | Obere Str. 57 | Berlin | 12209 | Germany |
| 2 | Ana Trujillo Emparedados y helados | Ana Trujillo | Avda. de la Constitución 2222 | México D.F. | 05021 | Mexico |
| 3 | Antonio Moreno Taquería | Antonio Moreno | Mataderos 2312 | México D.F. | 05023 | Mexico |

"Suppliers" table:

| SupplierID | SupplierName | ContactName | Address | City | PostalCode | Country |
|---|---|---|---|---|---|---|
| 1 | Exotic Liquid | Charlotte Cooper | 49 Gilbert St. | London | EC1 4SD | UK |
| 2 | New Orleans Cajun Delights | Shelley Burke | P.O. Box 78934 | New Orleans | 70117 | USA |
| 3 | Grandma Kelly's Homestead | Regina Murphy | 707 Oxford Rd. | Ann Arbor | 48104 | USA |

In order to select all different cities, distinct values, from the both the "Customers" and the "Suppliers" tables, use the following statement:

*SELECT City FROM Customers*

*UNION*

*SELECT City FROM Suppliers*

*ORDER BY City;*

Keep in mind that this does not provide data on duplicate cities and a city will only appear once, even if the tables share the same city. However, you can use UNION ALL in order to also return duplicate values.

**UNION ALL Example:**

In order to return all values, including duplicates, from both the "Customers" and "Suppliers" table, use the following SQL statement:

*SELECT City FROM Customers*

*UNION ALL*

*SELECT City FROM Suppliers*

*ORDER BY City;*

**UNION ALL with WHERE Example:**

In order to select all german cities, including duplicates, from both "Customers" and "Suppliers" tables, use the following statement:

*SELECT City, Country FROM Customers*

*WHERE Country='Germany'*

*UNION ALL*

*SELECT City, Country FROM Suppliers*

*WHERE Country='Germany'*
*ORDER BY City;*

Number of Records: 14

| City | Country |
|---|---|
| Aachen | Germany |
| Berlin | Germany |
| Berlin | Germany |
| Brandenburg | Germany |
| Cunewalde | Germany |
| Cuxhaven | Germany |
| Frankfurt | Germany |
| Frankfurt a.M. | Germany |
| Köln | Germany |
| Leipzig | Germany |
| Mannheim | Germany |
| München | Germany |
| Münster | Germany |
| Stuttgart | Germany |

# Chapter 25: SQL Select Into

With SQL SELECT INTO statement is used to copy/transfer data from one table in order to insert it into a new table.

**SQL SELECT INTO Syntax:**

You can copy all columns:

*SELECT ***

*INTO newtable [IN externaldb]*

*FROM table1;*

Or you can copy specific columns:

*SELECT column_name(s)*

*INTO newtable [IN externaldb]*

*FROM table1;*

The new table that is created will be done so with the column-names and the types that were defined in the SELECT statement. You can then, using the AS clause, apply new names.

**SELECT INTO Examples:**

First, create a backup copy of Customers:

*SELECT ***

*INTO CustomersBackup2013*

*FROM Customers;*

Then, use the IN clause to copy the table into another database:

*SELECT ***

*INTO CustomersBackup2013 IN 'Backup.mdb'*

*FROM Customers;*

In order to copy just a few columns into the new table:

*SELECT CustomerName, ContactName*

*INTO CustomersBackup2013*

*FROM Customers;*

In order to copy just German customers into the new table:

*SELECT ***

>    INTO CustomersBackup2013
>
>    FROM Customers
>
>    WHERE Country='Germany';

Then, copy data from more than one table into the new table:

>    SELECT Customers.CustomerName, Orders.OrderID
>
>    INTO CustomersOrderBackup2013
>
>    FROM Customers
>
>    LEFT JOIN Orders
>
>    ON Customers.CustomerID=Orders.CustomerID;

You can also use SELECT INTO in order to create a new and empty table by adding a WHERE clause in order to return no data. You can do so using the following statement:

>    SELECT *
>
>    INTO newtable
>
>    FROM table1
>
>    WHERE 1=0;

# Chapter 26: SQL Insert Into Select

If you want to copy data from one table into an existing table you can use the INSERT INTO SELECT. Doing it this way will not affect the existing rows in the target table.

**SQL INSERT INTO SELECT Syntax:**

In order to copy all columns:

> INSERT INTO table2
>
> SELECT * FROM table1;

Or we can copy only the columns we want to into another, existing table:

> INSERT INTO table2
>
> (column_name(s))
>
> SELECT column_name(s)
>
> FROM table1;

**INSERT INTO SELECT Example:**

"Customers" table:

| CustomerID | CustomerName | Contact Name | Address | City | PostalCode | Country |
|---|---|---|---|---|---|---|
| 1 | Alfreds Futterkiste | Maria Anders | Obere Str. 57 | Berlin | 12209 | Germany |
| 2 | Ana Trujillo Emparedados y helados | Ana Trujillo | Avda. de la Constitución 2222 | México D.F. | 05021 | Mexico |
| 3 | Antonio Moreno Taqueria | Antonio Moreno | Mataderos 2312 | México D.F. | 05023 | Mexico |

"Supplier" table:

| SupplierID | SupplierName | ContactName | Address | City | Postal Code | Country | Phone |
|---|---|---|---|---|---|---|---|
| 1 | Exotic Liquid | Charlotte Cooper | 49 Gilbert St. | Londona | EC1 4SD | UK | (171) 555-2222 |
| 2 | New Orleans Cajun Delights | Shelley Burke | P.O. Box 78934 | New Orleans | 70117 | USA | (100) 555-4822 |
| 3 | Grandma Kelly's Homestead | Regina Murphy | 707 Oxford Rd. | Ann Arbor | 48104 | USA | (313) 555-5735 |

To copy specific columns from "Suppliers" into "Customers" use the following statement:

*INSERT INTO Customers (CustomerName, Country)*

*SELECT SupplierName, Country FROM Suppliers;*

Your results will look like this:

*You have made changes to the database. Rows affected: 29*

In order to copy just German suppliers to the "Customers" table, use the following statement:

*INSERT INTO Customers (CustomerName, Country)*

*SELECT SupplierName, Country FROM Suppliers*

*WHERE Country='Germany';*

# Chapter 27: SQL Create DB

The SQL CREATE DATABASE Statement is used in order to create a new database.

**SQL CREATE DATABASE Syntax:**

*CREATE DATABASE dbname;*

**SQL CREATE DATABASE Example:**

This SQL statement will create a database titled "my db":

*CREATE DATABASE my_db;*

You can then add tables to the database using the CREATE TABLE statement.

# Chapter 28: SQL Create Table

The CREATE TABLE statement is used to create a new table within a database. Each table must be organized into rows and columns and must be named.

**SQL CREATE TABLE Syntax:**

*CREATE TABLE table_name*

*(*

*column_name1 data_type(size),*

*column_name2 data_type(size),*

*column_name3 data_type(size),*

*....*

*);*

The column name parameters are used to name each column of the table. The data type parameter is used to specify what kind of data the column can hold, ei varchar, integer, decimal, date, etc. The size parameter determines the maximum length of a column.

**CREATE TABLE Example:**

To create a table called "Persons" which contains five columns, each titled PersonID, LastName, FirstName, Address, and City, you can use the following statement:

*CREATE TABLE Persons*

*(*

*PersonID int,*

*LastName varchar(255),*

*FirstName varchar(255),*

*Address varchar(255),*

*City varchar(255)*

*);*

The PersonID column will hold an integer, and the remaining columns will contain characters, all with a maximum length of 255 characters. The created table will look like this:

| PersonID | LastName | FirstName | Address | City |
|----------|----------|-----------|---------|------|
|          |          |           |         |      |

You can then fill the table using the INSERT INTO statement.

# Chapter 29: SQL Constraints

SQL constraints are used in order to specify the rules for the data that a table contains. They can be specified during or after a table's creation. This can be done with the CREATE TABLE and ALTER TABLE statements respectively.

**SQL CREATE TABLE + CONSTRAINT Syntax:**

*CREATE TABLE table_name*

*(*

*column_name1 data_type(size) constraint_name,*

*column_name2 data_type(size) constraint_name,*

*column_name3 data_type(size) constraint_name,*

*....*

*);*

- Here is a list of constraints that can be specified:
- NOT NULL - column cannot store a NULL value.
- UNIQUE - Ensures that each row in a column contains a unique value
- PRIMARY KEY - This is a combination of NOT NULL and UNIQUE. This ensures that a column, or multiple columns, have a unique identity.
- FOREIGN KEY - Maintains the referential integrity of one table's data to match another table's values.
- CHECK - Ensures that a value in a column meets specific conditions.
- DEFAULT - Specifies a column's default value

Constraints will be covered in more detail in the following chapters.

# Chapter 30: SQL Not Null

A table column will be able to hold NULL values by default. To change this, and to make it so that a table's column does not accept NULL values, you must use a SQL NOT NULL Constraint. Doing so makes it so that you cannot add a new record or update an existing record without adding a value into the constrained field.

**NOT NULL example:**

CREATE TABLE PersonsNotNull

(

P_Id int NOT NULL,

LastName varchar(255) NOT NULL,

FirstName varchar(255),

Address varchar(255),

City varchar(255)

)

# Chapter 31: SQL Unique

A SQL UNIQUE constraint is used so the each record in a table can be uniquely identified. This, as well as the PRIMARY KEY, will guarantee uniqueness for one or multiple columns. A PRIMARY KEY constraint automatically has a UNIQUE constraint defined within it. It is important to know that you can only have one PRIMARY KEY constraint per table, whereas you can have multiple UNIQUE constraints.

**UNIQUE Constraint on CREATE TABLE:**

In order to add a UNIQUE constraint on the "P Id" column once "Persons" table is created, use this statement (works for SQL Server, Oracle, and MS Access):

> CREATE TABLE Persons
>
> (
>
> P_Id int NOT NULL UNIQUE,
>
> LastName varchar(255) NOT NULL,
>
> FirstName varchar(255),
>
> Address varchar(255),
>
> City varchar(255)
>
> )

For MySQL, use this:

> CREATE TABLE Persons
>
> (
>
> P_Id int NOT NULL,
>
> LastName varchar(255) NOT NULL,
>
> FirstName varchar(255),
>
> Address varchar(255),
>
> City varchar(255),
>
> UNIQUE (P_Id)
>
> )

To name or define a UNIQUE constraint on multiple columns, you can use this (works for MySQL, SQL Server, Oracle, and MS Access):

```
CREATE TABLE Persons
(
P_Id int NOT NULL,
LastName varchar(255) NOT NULL,
FirstName varchar(255),
Address varchar(255),
City varchar(255),
CONSTRAINT uc_PersonID UNIQUE (P_Id,LastName)
)
```

In order to create a UNIQUE constraint on the "P Id" column on a pre-existing "Persons" table, use the following (works for MySQL, SQL Server, Oracle, and MS ACCESS):

```
ALTER TABLE Persons
ADD UNIQUE (P_Id)
```

To do the same, but with multiple columns, use the following:

```
ALTER TABLE Persons
ADD CONSTRAINT uc_PersonID UNIQUE (P_Id,LastName)
```

To remove or DROP a UNIQUE constraint, use the following for MySQL:

```
ALTER TABLE Persons
DROP INDEX uc_PersonID
```

For SQL Server, Oracle, and MS Access, use the following:

```
ALTER TABLE Persons
DROP CONSTRAINT uc_PersonID
```

# Chapter 32: SQL Primary Key

The PRIMARY KEY constraint is used in order to uniquely identify each record within a table. They have to contain UNIQUE values. A PRIMARY KEY column cannot contain NULL values. Each table can only have one primary key, and most tables should have it.

In order to create a PRIMARY KEY on the "P_Id" column during the creation of the "Persons" table, use the following (for MySQL):

> CREATE TABLE Persons
>
> (
>
> P_Id int NOT NULL,
>
> LastName varchar(255) NOT NULL,
>
> FirstName varchar(255),
>
> Address varchar(255),
>
> City varchar(255),
>
> PRIMARY KEY (P_Id)
>
> )

For SQL Server, Oracle, and MS Access, use the following:

> CREATE TABLE Persons
>
> (
>
> P_Id int NOT NULL PRIMARY KEY,
>
> LastName varchar(255) NOT NULL,
>
> FirstName varchar(255),
>
> Address varchar(255),
>
> City varchar(255)
>
> )

In order to name or define a PRIMARY KEY on multiple columns, use the following (for MySQL, SQL Server, Oracle, and MS Access):

> CREATE TABLE Persons
>
> (
>
> P_Id int NOT NULL,

*LastName varchar(255) NOT NULL,*

*FirstName varchar(255),*

*Address varchar(255),*

*City varchar(255),*

*CONSTRAINT pk_PersonID PRIMARY KEY (P_Id,LastName)*

*)*

In order to add a PRIMARY KEY constraint on the "P Id" column for a pre-existing "Persons" table, use the following (for MySQL, SQL Server, Oracle, and MS Access):

*ALTER TABLE Persons*

*ADD PRIMARY KEY (P_Id)*

To do the same with multiple columns, use the following (for MySQL, SQL Server, Oracle, and MS Access):

*ALTER TABLE Persons*

*ADD CONSTRAINT pk_PersonID PRIMARY KEY (P_Id,LastName)*

In order to delete, or DROP a PRIMARY KEY constraint, use the following (for MySQL):

*ALTER TABLE Persons*

*DROP PRIMARY KEY*

For SQL Server, Oracle, and MS Access, use the following:

*ALTER TABLE Persons*

*DROP CONSTRAINT pk_PersonID*

# Chapter 33: SQL Foreign Key

The SQL FOREIGN KEY constraint is used in one table to point to a PRIMARY KEY in a different table. For example, look at the "Persons" table and the "Orders" table.

"Persons" table

| P_Id | LastName | FirstName | Address | City |
|---|---|---|---|---|
| 1 | Hansen | Ola | Timoteivn 10 | Sandnes |
| 2 | Svendson | Tove | Borgvn 23 | Sandnes |
| 3 | Pettersen | Kari | Storgt 20 | Stavanger |

"Orders" table

| O_Id | OrderNo | P_Id |
|---|---|---|
| 1 | 77895 | 3 |
| 2 | 44678 | 3 |
| 3 | 22456 | 2 |
| 4 | 24562 | 1 |

For this example, the "P_Id" column, the FOREIGN KEY, in the "Orders" table is pointing to the "P_Id" column, which is the PRIMARY KEY for our "Persons" table. The FOREIGN KEY constraint also prevents the insertion of invalid data into the applied column. This is because it has to be one of the values contained in that table that the FOREIGN KEY points to.

In order to create a FOREIGN KEY on the "P_Id" column upon the creation of the "Orders" table, use the following (for MySQL):

*CREATE TABLE Orders*

*(*

*O_Id int NOT NULL,*

*OrderNo int NOT NULL,*

*P_Id int,*

*PRIMARY KEY (O_Id),*

FOREIGN KEY (P_Id) REFERENCES Persons(P_Id)
)

For SQL Server, Oracle, MS Access, use the following:

CREATE TABLE Orders
(
O_Id int NOT NULL PRIMARY KEY,
OrderNo int NOT NULL,
P_Id int FOREIGN KEY REFERENCES Persons(P_Id)
)

In order to do the same with multiple columns, use the following (for MySQL, SQL Server, Oracle, and MS Access):

CREATE TABLE Orders
(
O_Id int NOT NULL,
OrderNo int NOT NULL,
P_Id int,
PRIMARY KEY (O_Id),
CONSTRAINT fk_PerOrders FOREIGN KEY (P_Id)
REFERENCES Persons(P_Id)
)

In order to add a FOREIGN KEY constraint on the "P Id" column for a pre-existing "Orders" table, use the following (for MySQL, SQL Server, Oracle, and MS Access):

ALTER TABLE Orders
ADD FOREIGN KEY (P_Id)
REFERENCES Persons(P_Id)

In order to do the same with multiple columns, use the following (for MySQL, SQL Server, Oracle, and MS Access):

ALTER TABLE Orders
ADD CONSTRAINT fk_PerOrders
FOREIGN KEY (P_Id)

*REFERENCES Persons(P_Id)*

In order to delete or DROP a FOREIGN KEY constraint use the following (for MySQL):

*ALTER TABLE Orders*

*DROP FOREIGN KEY fk_PerOrders*

For SQL Server, Oracle, and MS Access, use the following:

*ALTER TABLE Orders*

*DROP CONSTRAINT fk_PerOrders*

# Chapter 34: SQL Check

The SQL CHECK Constraint can be used to only allow certain values in a single column or, when on a table, limits values in certain values based on values in other columns in that row.

In order to create a CHECK constraint that will specify that a column must only include integers that are greater than 0 on the "P Id" column during the construction of the "Persons" table creation, use the following (for MySQL):

CREATE TABLE Persons

(

P_Id int NOT NULL,

LastName varchar(255) NOT NULL,

FirstName varchar(255),

Address varchar(255),

City varchar(255),

CHECK (P_Id>0)

)

For SQL Server, Oracle, and MS Access, use the following:

CREATE TABLE Persons

(

P_Id int NOT NULL CHECK (P_Id>0),

LastName varchar(255) NOT NULL,

FirstName varchar(255),

Address varchar(255),

City varchar(255)

)

In order to do the same with multiple columns, use the following (for MySQL, SQL Server, Oracle, and MS Access):

CREATE TABLE Persons

(

P_Id int NOT NULL,

*LastName varchar(255) NOT NULL,*

*FirstName varchar(255),*

*Address varchar(255),*

*City varchar(255),*

*CONSTRAINT chk_Person CHECK (P_Id>0 AND City='Sandnes')*

*)*

In order to add a FOREIGN KEY constraint on the "P_Id" column for a pre-existing "Persons" table, use the following (for MySQL, SQL Server, Oracle, and MS Access):

*ALTER TABLE Persons*

*ADD CHECK (P_Id>0)*

To do the same with multiple columns, use the following (for MySQL, SQL Server, Oracle, MS Access):

*ALTER TABLE Persons*

*ADD CONSTRAINT chk_Person CHECK (P_Id>0 AND City='Sandnes')*

In order to delete or DROP a CHECK constraint, use the following (for SQL Server, Oracle, and MS Access):

*ALTER TABLE Persons*

*DROP CONSTRAINT chk_Person*

For MySQL, use the following:

*ALTER TABLE Persons*

*DROP CHECK chk_Person*

# Chapter 35: SQL Default

The SQL Default constraint is used in order to add a default value to a column, which will be added to each new record if no other value is specified.

To create a DEFAULT constraint in the "City" column curing the creation of the "Persons" table, use the following (for MySQL, SQL Server, Oracle, and MS Access):

> CREATE TABLE Persons
>
> (
>
> P_Id int NOT NULL,
>
> LastName varchar(255) NOT NULL,
>
> FirstName varchar(255),
>
> Address varchar(255),
>
> City varchar(255) DEFAULT 'Sandnes'
>
> )

You can also utilize the DEFAULT constraint in order to utilize system values by using constructions like GETDATE():

> CREATE TABLE Orders
>
> (
>
> O_Id int NOT NULL,
>
> OrderNo int NOT NULL,
>
> P_Id int,
>
> OrderDate date DEFAULT GETDATE()
>
> )

In order to add a DEFAULT constraint on the "P Id" column for a pre-existing "Persons" table, use the following (for MySQL):

> ALTER TABLE Persons
>
> ALTER City SET DEFAULT 'SANDNES'

For SQL Server and MS Access, use the following:

> ALTER TABLE Persons
>
> ALTER COLUMN City SET DEFAULT 'SANDNES'

For Oracle, use the following:

> *ALTER TABLE Persons*
>
> *MODIFY City DEFAULT 'SANDNES'*

In order to delete or DROP a DEFAULT constraint, use the following (for MySQL):

> *ALTER TABLE Persons*
>
> *ALTER City DROP DEFAULT*

For SQL Server, Oracle, or MS Access, use the following:

> *ALTER TABLE Persons*
>
> *ALTER COLUMN City DROP DEFAULT*

# Chapter 36: SQL Create Index

The SQL CREATE INDEX statement is used in order to create indexes in tables, which allow the database application to find data quickly, without having to scan the entire table. Users are not able to see indexes; they simply help to make searches quicker and more efficient. It is also important to understand that updating a table with indexes takes longer than updating tables without indexes. This is because the indexes must be updated as well. Because of this, indexes should only be created on columns and tables that are frequently searched against.

**SQL CREATE INDEX Syntax:**

This creates an index for a table, which allows duplicates.

*CREATE INDEX index_name*

*ON table_name (column_name)*

**SQL CREATE UNIQUE INDEX Syntax:**

This creates a unique index for a table, which does not allow duplicates.

*CREATE UNIQUE INDEX index_name*

*ON table_name (column_name)*

It is important to note that the syntax for creating indexes can vary between databases.

**CREATE INDEX Example:**

In order to create an index named "Pindes" on the "LastName" column on the "Persons" table" use the following statement:

*CREATE INDEX PIndex*

*ON Persons (LastName)*

You can do the same, with multiple columns, by listing the column names within parentheses, and separated by commas using a statement similar to this:

*CREATE INDEX PIndex*

*ON Persons (LastName, FirstName)*

# Chapter 37: SQL Drop

A SQL DROP statement can be used to easily delete or remove indexes, tables, and databases.

The DROP INDEX statement is used to remove or delete an index within a table.

**DROP INDEX Syntax (MS Access):**

*DROP INDEX index_name ON table_name*

**DROP INDEX Syntax (MS SQL Server):**

*DROP INDEX table_name.index_name*

**DROP INDEX Syntax (DB2/Oracle):**

*DROP INDEX index_name*

**DROP INDEX Syntax (MySQL):**

*ALTER TABLE table_name DROP INDEX index_name*

The DROP TABLE statement is for removing or deleting a table from a database.

*DROP TABLE table_name*

The DROP DATABASE statement is used to remove or delete a database.

*DROP DATABASE database_name*

If you want to delete all of the data within a table, but leave the table intact, you can use the TRUNCATE TABLE statement.

*TRUNCATE TABLE table_name*

# Chapter 38: SQL Alter

The SQL ALTER TABLE statement is used in order to add, delete or modify the columns of an existing table.

**SQL ALTER TABLE Syntax:**

In order to add a column to a table, use the following:

*ALTER TABLE table_name*

*ADD column_name datatype*

In order to delete a specific column from a table (which some databases do not allow), use the following:

*ALTER TABLE table_name*

*DROP COLUMN column_name*

To change the type of data of a column in a table, use the following (for SQL Server and MS Access):

*ALTER TABLE table_name*

*ALTER COLUMN column_name datatype*

For My SQL and Oracle (prior version 10G), use the following:

*ALTER TABLE table_name*

*MODIFY COLUMN column_name datatype*

For Oracle 10G and later, use the following:

*ALTER TABLE table_name*

*MODIFY column_name datatype*

**ALTER TABLE Example:**

To begin, look at the "Persons" table.

| P_Id | LastName | FirstName | Address | City |
|---|---|---|---|---|
| 1 | Hansen | Ola | Timoteivn 10 | Sandnes |
| 2 | Svendson | Tove | Borgvn 23 | Sandnes |
| 3 | Pettersen | Kari | Storgt 20 | Stavanger |

If you want to add a "DateOfBirth" column to the table, you can use the following:

*ALTER TABLE Persons*

*ADD DateOfBirth date*

Note that the data type for the "DateOfBirth" column is the type of date, and will hold a date.

The change will appear like this:

| P_Id | LastName | FirstName | Address | City | DateOfBirth |
|---|---|---|---|---|---|
| 1 | Hansen | Ola | Timoteivn 10 | Sandnes | |
| 2 | Svendson | Tove | Borgvn 23 | Sandnes | |
| 3 | Pettersen | Kari | Storgt 20 | Stavanger | |

If you want to change the type of data that the "DateOfBirth" column can hold, use the following:

*ALTER TABLE Persons*

*ALTER COLUMN DateOfBirth year*

The "DateOfBirth" column will now only contain a year in either a two or four digit format, rather than a full date.

Now if you want to remove or delete the "DateOfBirth" column from the "Persons" table, use the following:

*ALTER TABLE Persons*

*DROP COLUMN DateOfBirth*

The change will now look like this:

| P_Id | LastName | FirstName | Address | City |
|---|---|---|---|---|
| 1 | Hansen | Ola | Timoteivn 10 | Sandnes |
| 2 | Svendson | Tove | Borgvn 23 | Sandnes |
| 3 | Pettersen | Kari | Storgt 20 | Stavanger |

# Chapter 39: SQL Auto Increment

The SQL auto-increment allows unique numbers to generate for new records added to a table.

AUTO INCREMENT Field

Commonly you would like for the value of the PRIMARY KEY field to be created automatically each time a record is inserted.

**Syntax For MySQL:**

In order to define the "ID" column to be an AUTO_INCREMENT PRIMARY KEY field in the "Persons" table, use this statement:

> CREATE TABLE Persons
>
> (
>
> ID int NOT NULL AUTO_INCREMENT,
>
> LastName varchar(255) NOT NULL,
>
> FirstName varchar(255),
>
> Address varchar(255),
>
> City varchar(255),
>
> PRIMARY KEY (ID)
>
> )

By default, MySQL has a starting value of 1 and will increase by 1 for each new record. To have the sequence start with another value, you can use the following:

> ALTER TABLE Persons AUTO_INCREMENT=100

As we have previously seen, adding a new record to the "Persons" will automatically fill out the "ID" column.

**Syntax for SQL Server:**

To define the "ID" column as an auto-incremented PRIMARY KEY field in the "Persons" table, use the following:

> CREATE TABLE Persons
>
> (
>
> ID int IDENTITY(1,1) PRIMARY KEY,
>
> LastName varchar(255) NOT NULL,

*FirstName varchar(255),*

*Address varchar(255),*

*City varchar(255)*

*)*

The MS SQL Server uses the IDENTITY keyword in order to accomplish the auto-increment feature. In order to start at 10, and increase by 5, use IDENTITY (10,5)

**Syntax for Access:**

In order to utilize the auto-increment feature for the "ID" column in the "Persons" table, use the following:

*CREATE TABLE Persons*

*(*

*ID Integer PRIMARY KEY AUTOINCREMENT,*

*LastName varchar(255) NOT NULL,*

*FirstName varchar(255),*

*Address varchar(255),*

*City varchar(255)*

*)*

MS Access uses the AUTOINCREMENT keyword to perform the feature. In order to start at 10 and increase by 5, use AUTOINCREMENT(10,5)

**Syntax for Oracle:**

Auto-incrementing in Oracle can be tricky. You will first have to create a sequence object to generate the number sequence. To do so, use this CREATE SEQUENCE syntax:

*CREATE SEQUENCE seq_person*

*MINVALUE 1*

*START WITH 1*

*INCREMENT BY 1*

*CACHE 10*

This creates an object called seq_person, that starts with 1 and increases by 1. It can also cache up to 10 values for increased performance. The cache option will specify the number of sequence values that can be stored.

Next, to insert a record into the "Persons" table, you will use the nextval function, which retrieves the next value from seq_person:

*INSERT INTO Persons (ID,FirstName,LastName)*

*VALUES (seq_person.nextval,'Lars','Monsen')*

# Chapter 40: SQL Views

A view is a virtual table that is based on a result set of a statement, which contains rows and columns, much like a real table. The view covers fields from one or more real tables in a database. You can add functions, WHERE, and JOIN statements to a view in order to present the data like it was coming from a single table.

**SQL CREATE VIEW Syntax:**

> CREATE VIEW view_name AS
>
> SELECT column_name(s)
>
> FROM table_name
>
> WHERE condition

**SQL CREATE VIEW Examples:**

By default, the Northwind database has several views installed. The "Current Product List" view will list all active products from the "Products" table. It is created with the following:

> CREATE VIEW [Current Product List] AS
>
> SELECT ProductID,ProductName
>
> FROM Products
>
> WHERE Discontinued=No

You can query that view like this:

> SELECT * FROM [Current Product List]

An alternate view within the Northwind sample database will select every product within the "Products" table with a higher than average price:

> CREATE VIEW [Products Above Average Price] AS
>
> SELECT ProductName,UnitPrice
>
> FROM Products
>
> WHERE UnitPrice>(SELECT AVG(UnitPrice) FROM Products)

You can query that view like this:

> SELECT * FROM [Products Above Average Price]

Yet another view in the Northwind Database will calculate the total sales of each category in 1997. This view will select data from a different view called "Product Sales for 1997":

> CREATE VIEW [Category Sales For 1997] AS
>
> SELECT DISTINCT CategoryName,Sum(ProductSales) AS CategorySales
>
> FROM [Product Sales for 1997]
>
> GROUP BY CategoryName

You can query that view like this:

> SELECT * FROM [Category Sales For 1997]

You can also add additional conditions to the queries. For example, you can see total sales for "Beverages alone":

> SELECT * FROM [Category Sales For 1997]
>
> WHERE CategoryName='Beverages'

## SQL Updating a View:

Update a view by using the following:

> CREATE OR REPLACE VIEW view_name AS
>
> SELECT column_name(s)
>
> FROM table_name
>
> WHERE condition

To add a "Category" column to the "Current Product List" view, you will update with the following:

> CREATE OR REPLACE VIEW [Current Product List] AS
>
> SELECT ProductID,ProductName,Category
>
> FROM Products
>
> WHERE Discontinued=No

## SQL Dropping a View:

This can be done with the DROP VIEW command,

> DROP VIEW view_name

# Chapter 41: SQL Dates

When working with dates, the most difficult task can be making sure that you are using the proper format, as it has to match the format of the date column. As long as the data only contains the date portion, queries will go as expected. On the other hand, if a time portion is included, complications can arise. Before getting into complications, let's look at some important built-in functions when working with dates.

Here are the most important built-in date functions in MySQL:

| Function | Description |
| --- | --- |
| NOW() | Returns the current date and time |
| CURDATE() | Returns the current date |
| CURTIME() | Returns the current time |
| DATE() | Extracts the date part of a date or date/time expression |
| EXTRACT() | Returns a single part of a date/time |
| DATE_ADD() | Adds a specified time interval to a date |
| DATE_SUB() | Subtracts a specified time interval from a date |
| DATEDIFF() | Returns the number of days between two dates |
| DATE_FORMAT() | Displays date/time data in different formats |

Here are the most important built-in date functions in MySQL:

| Function | Description |
| --- | --- |
| GETDATE() | Returns the current date and time |
| DATEPART() | Returns a single part of a date/time |
| DATEADD() | Adds or subtracts a specified time interval from a date |
| DATEDIFF() | Returns the time between two dates |
| CONVERT() | Displays date/time data in different formats |

**SQL Date Data Types:**

MySQL Date Data Types:

- DATE - format YYYY-MM-DD
- DATETIME - format: YYYY-MM-DD HH:MI:SS
- TIMESTAMP - format: YYYY-MM-DD HH:MI:SS
- YEAR - format YYYY or YY

SQL Server Date Data Types:

- DATE - format YYYY-MM-DD
- DATETIME - format: YYYY-MM-DD HH:MI:SS
- SMALLDATETIME - format: YYYY-MM-DD HH:MI:SS
- TIMESTAMP - format: a unique number

It is important to understand that date types are chosen upon the creation of a new table in a database.

It is really easy to compare dates as long as there is no time component.

"Orders" table:

| OrderId | ProductName | OrderDate |
|---------|-------------|-----------|
| 1 | Geitost | 2008-11-11 |
| 2 | Camembert Pierrot | 2008-11-09 |
| 3 | Mozzarella di Giovanni | 2008-11-11 |
| 4 | Mascarpone Fabioli | 2008-10-29 |

In order to select records with the OrderDate of "2008-11-11" from the above table, we will use the following:

*SELECT \* FROM Orders WHERE OrderDate='2008-11-11'*

Which would give this result:

| OrderId | ProductName | OrderDate |
|---------|-------------|-----------|
| 1 | Geitost | 2008-11-11 |
| 3 | Mozzarella di Giovanni | 2008-11-11 |

Now, look at this "Orders" table containing time.

| OrderId | ProductName | OrderDate |
|---|---|---|
| 1 | Geitost | 2008-11-11 13:23:44 |
| 2 | Camembert Pierrot | 2008-11-09 15:45:21 |
| 3 | Mozzarella di Giovanni | 2008-11-11 11:12:01 |
| 4 | Mascarpone Fabioli | 2008-10-29 14:56:59 |

Using the same statement as before will return no results. That is because the time portion is not included. If you have the option, do not include a time portion in your date.

# Chapter 42: SQL Null Values

NULL values represent missing or unknown data, which table columns can contain by default. In this chapter, we will explain IS NULL and IS NOT NULL operators.

If a column is optional, you can update an existing or add a new record without adding a value, which means that the field will be saved with a NULL value. These are treated differently from other values and are used as a placeholder. NULL is not equal to 0.

Look at the following "Persons" table:

| P_Id | LastName | FirstName | Address | City |
|---|---|---|---|---|
| 1 | Hansen | Ola | | Sandnes |
| 2 | Svendson | Tove | Borgvn 23 | Sandnes |
| 3 | Pettersen | Kari | | Stavanger |

If the "Address" column is optional, and no record is inserted for that column, the the "Address" column will be saved as NULL.

So how can you test for NULL values? To do so, you can not use comparison operators, like =,<, or <>. Instead, you will have to use IS NULL or IS NOT NULL operators.

**SQL IS NULL:**

To select only records containing a NULL value in the "Address" column, use the IS NULL operator:

> SELECT LastName,FirstName,Address FROM Persons
>
> WHERE Address IS NULL

This will result in a return like this:

| LastName | FirstName | Address |
|---|---|---|
| Hansen | Ola | |
| Pettersen | Kari | |

**SQL IS NOT NULL:**

To select only records with no NULL value in the "Address" column, use the IS NOT NULL operator:

*SELECT LastName,FirstName,Address FROM Persons*
*WHERE Address IS NOT NULL*

This will result in a return like this:

| LastName | FirstName | Address |
|---|---|---|
| Svendson | Tove | Borgvn 23 |

# Chapter 43: SQL Null Functions

This chapter will go over NULL functions, ISNULL(), NVL(), IFNULL, and COALESCE() Functions.

"Products" table:

| P_Id | ProductName | UnitPrice | UnitsInStock | UnitsOnOrder |
|---|---|---|---|---|
| 1 | Jarlsberg | 10.45 | 16 | 15 |
| 2 | Mascarpone | 32.56 | 23 | |
| 3 | Gorgonzola | 15.67 | 9 | 20 |

If the "UnitsOnOrder" column is optional and might contain NULL values, you can use the following:

> SELECT ProductName,UnitPrice*(UnitsInStock+UnitsOnOrder)
>
> FROM Products

In this example, in there are an NULL values in "UnitsOnOrder", then the result is NULL. Microsoft's ISNULL() function specifies how we want to treat NULL values. The NVL(), IFNULL(), and COALESCE() functions can achieve the same results.

Assume we want NULL values to be zeros. If "UnitsOnOrder" is NULL, then the calculation will not be harmed. This is because ISNULL() returns a zero if the value is NULL:

**For MS AccessL**

> SELECT ProductName,UnitPrice*(UnitsInStock+IIF(ISNULL(UnitsOnOrder),0,UnitsOnOrder))
>
> FROM Products

**For SQL Server:**

> SELECT ProductName,UnitPrice*(UnitsInStock+ISNULL(UnitsOnOrder,0))
>
> FROM Products

**For Oracle:**

There is no ISNULL() function in Oracle, however, you can use NVL() function to obtain the same result:

*SELECT ProductName,UnitPrice\*(UnitsInStock+NVL(UnitsOnOrder,0))*

*FROM Products*

**For MySQL:**

The ISNULL() function works different for MySQL works differently from Microsofts. In MySQL we can use the IFNULL() function:

*SELECT ProductName,UnitPrice\*(UnitsInStock+IFNULL(UnitsOnOrder, 0))*

*FROM Products*

or use COALESCE() function:

*SELECT ProductName,UnitPrice\*(UnitsInStock+COALESCE(UnitsOnOrder,0))*

*FROM Products*

# Chapter 44: SQL Data Types

Data types define the type of value contained in a column. Each column in a database table requires a name and data type.

Here is a list of the general data types used in SQL:

| Data type | Description |
|---|---|
| CHARACTER(n) | Character string. Fixed-length n |
| VARCHAR(n) or CHARACTER VARYING(n) | Character string. Variable length. Maximum length n |
| BINARY(n) | Binary string. Fixed-length n |
| BOOLEAN | Stores TRUE or FALSE values |
| VARBINARY(n) or BINARY VARYING(n) | Binary string. Variable length. Maximum length n |
| INTEGER(p) | Integer numerical (no decimal). Precision p |
| SMALLINT | Integer numerical (no decimal). Precision 5 |
| INTEGER | Integer numerical (no decimal). Precision 10 |
| BIGINT | Integer numerical (no decimal). Precision 19 |
| DECIMAL(p,s) | Exact numerical, precision p, scale s. Example: decimal(5,2) is a number that has 3 digits before the decimal and 2 digits after the decimal |
| NUMERIC(p,s) | Exact numerical, precision p, scale s. (Same as DECIMAL) |
| FLOAT(p) | Approximate numerical, mantissa precision p. A floating number in base 10 exponential notation. The size argument for this type consists of a single number specifying the minimum precision |
| REAL | Approximate numerical, mantissa precision 7 |
| FLOAT | Approximate numerical, mantissa precision 16 |

| | |
|---|---|
| DOUBLE PRECISION | Approximate numerical, mantissa precision 16 |
| DATE | Stores year, month, and day values |
| TIME | Stores hour, minute, and second values |
| TIMESTAMP | Stores year, month, day, hour, minute, and second values |
| INTERVAL | Composed of a number of integer fields, representing a period of time, depending on the type of interval |
| ARRAY | A set-length and ordered collection of elements |
| MULTISET | A variable-length and unordered collection of elements |
| XML | Stores XML data |

Different databases have different options for data type definition. Here are some common data types by various platforms:

| Data type | Access | SQL Server | Oracle | MySQL | PostgreSQL |
|---|---|---|---|---|---|
| boolean | Yes/No | Bit | Byte | N/A | Boolean |
| integer | Number (integer) | Int | Number | Int Integer | Int Integer |
| float | Number (single) | Float Real | Number | Float | Numeric |
| currency | Currency | Money | N/A | N/A | Money |
| string (fixed) | N/A | Char | Char | Char | Char |
| string (variable) | Text (<256) Memo (65k+) | Varchar | Varchar Varchar2 | Varchar | Varchar |
| binary object | OLE Object Memo | Binary (fixed up to 8K) Varbinary (<8K) Image (<2GB) | Long Raw | Blob Text | Binary Varbinary |

136

# Chapter 45: SQL DB Data Types

**Here is a list of data types for Microsoft Access:**

| Data type | Description | Storage |
|---|---|---|
| Text | Use for text or combinations of text and numbers. 255 characters maximum | |
| Memo | Memo is used for larger amounts of text. Stores up to 65,536 characters. Note: You cannot sort a memo field. However, they are searchable | |
| Byte | Allows whole numbers from 0 to 255 | 1 byte |
| Integer | Allows whole numbers between -32,768 and 32,767 | 2 bytes |
| Long | Allows whole numbers between -2,147,483,648 and 2,147,483,647 | 4 bytes |
| Single | Single precision floating-point. Will handle most decimals | 4 bytes |
| Double | Double precision floating-point. Will handle most decimals | 8 bytes |
| Currency | Use for currency. Holds up to 15 digits of whole dollars, plus 4 decimal places. Tip: You can choose which country's currency to use | 8 bytes |
| AutoNumber | AutoNumber fields automatically give each record its own number, usually starting at 1 | 4 bytes |
| Date/Time | Use for dates and times | 8 bytes |
| Yes/No | A logical field can be displayed as Yes/No, True/False, or On/Off. In code, use the constants True and False (equivalent to -1 and 0). Note: Null values are not allowed in Yes/No fields | 1 bit |
| Ole Object | Can store pictures, audio, video, or other BLOBs (Binary Large OBjects) | up to 1GB |

**Here is a list of data types for MySQL**: (which contains three main types: text, number, and date/time types)

Text:

| Data type | Description |
|---|---|
| CHAR(size) | Holds a fixed length string (can contain letters, numbers, and special characters). The fixed size is specified in parenthesis. Can store up to 255 characters |
| VARCHAR(size) | Holds a variable length string (can contain letters, numbers, and special characters). The maximum size is specified in parenthesis. Can store up to 255 characters. Note:If you put a greater value than 255 it will be converted to a TEXT type |
| TINYTEXT | Holds a string with a maximum length of 255 characters |
| TEXT | Holds a string with a maximum length of 65,535 characters |
| BLOB | For BLOBs (Binary Large OBjects). Holds up to 65,535 bytes of data |
| MEDIUMTEXT | Holds a string with a maximum length of 16,777,215 characters |
| MEDIUMBLOB | For BLOBs (Binary Large OBjects). Holds up to 16,777,215 bytes of data |
| LONGTEXT | Holds a string with a maximum length of 4,294,967,295 characters |
| LONGBLOB | For BLOBs (Binary Large OBjects). Holds up to 4,294,967,295 bytes of data |
| ENUM(x,y,z,etc.) | Let you enter a list of possible values. You can list up to 65535 values in an ENUM list. If a value is inserted that is not in the list, a blank value will be inserted.<br>Note: The values are sorted in the order you enter them.<br>You enter the possible values in this format: ENUM('X','Y','Z') |
| SET | Similar to ENUM except that SET may contain up to 64 list items and can store more than one choice |

Number:

| Data type | Description |
|---|---|
| TINYINT(size) | -128 to 127 normal. 0 to 255 UNSIGNED*. The maximum number of digits may be specified in parenthesis |
| SMALLINT(size) | -32768 to 32767 normal. 0 to 65535 UNSIGNED*. The maximum number of digits may be specified in parenthesis |
| MEDIUMINT(size) | -8388608 to 8388607 normal. 0 to 16777215 UNSIGNED*. The maximum number of digits may be specified in parenthesis |
| INT(size) | -2147483648 to 2147483647 normal. 0 to 4294967295 UNSIGNED*. The maximum number of digits may be specified in parenthesis |
| BIGINT(size) | -9223372036854775808 to 9223372036854775807 normal. 0 to 18446744073709551615 UNSIGNED*. The maximum number of digits may be specified in parenthesis |
| FLOAT(size,d) | A small number with a floating decimal point. The maximum number of digits may be specified in the size parameter. The maximum number of digits to the right of the decimal point is specified in the d parameter |
| DOUBLE(size,d) | A large number with a floating decimal point. The maximum number of digits may be specified in the size parameter. The maximum number of digits to the right of the decimal point is specified in the d parameter |
| DECIMAL(size,d) | A DOUBLE stored as a string, allowing for a fixed decimal point. The maximum number of digits may be specified in the size parameter. The maximum number of digits to the right of the decimal point is specified in the d parameter |

## Date:

| Data type | Description |
|---|---|
| DATE() | A date. Format: YYYY-MM-DD<br>Note: The supported range is from '1000-01-01' to '9999-12-31' |
| DATETIME() | *A date and time combination. Format: YYYY-MM-DD HH:MI:SS<br>Note: The supported range is from '1000-01-01 00:00:00' to '9999-12-31 23:59:59' |
| TIMESTAMP() | *A timestamp. TIMESTAMP values are stored as the number of seconds since the Unix epoch ('1970-01-01 00:00:00' UTC). Format: YYYY-MM-DD HH:MI:SS<br>Note: The supported range is from '1970-01-01 00:00:01' UTC to '2038-01-09 03:14:07' UTC |
| TIME() | A time. Format: HH:MI:SS<br>Note: The supported range is from '-838:59:59' to '838:59:59' |
| YEAR() | A year in two-digit or four-digit format.<br>Note: Values allowed in four-digit format: 1901 to 2155. Values allowed in two-digit format: 70 to 69, representing years from 1970 to 2069 |

# SQL Server Data Types:

## String:

| Data type | Description | Storage |
|---|---|---|
| char(n) | Fixed width character string. Maximum 8,000 characters | Defined width |
| varchar(n) | Variable width character string. Maximum 8,000 characters | 2 bytes + number of chars |
| varchar(max) | Variable width character string. Maximum 1,073,741,824 characters | 2 bytes + number of chars |
| text | Variable width character string. Maximum 2GB of text data | 4 bytes + number of chars |
| nchar | Fixed width Unicode string. Maximum 4,000 characters | Defined width x 2 |
| nvarchar | Variable width Unicode string. Maximum 4,000 characters | |
| nvarchar(max) | Variable width Unicode string. Maximum 536,870,912 characters | |
| ntext | Variable width Unicode string. Maximum 2GB of text data | |
| bit | Allows 0, 1, or NULL | |
| binary(n) | Fixed width binary string. Maximum 8,000 bytes | |
| varbinary | Variable width binary string. Maximum 8,000 bytes | |
| varbinary(max) | Variable width binary string. Maximum 2GB | |
| image | Variable width binary string. Maximum 2GB | |

## Number:

| Data type | Description | Storage |
|---|---|---|
| tinyint | Allows whole numbers from 0 to 255 | 1 byte |
| smallint | Allows whole numbers between -32,768 and 32,767 | 2 bytes |
| int | Allows whole numbers between -2,147,483,648 and 2,147,483,647 | 4 bytes |
| bigint | Allows whole numbers between -9,223,372,036,854,775,808 and 9,223,372,036,854,775,807 | 8 bytes |
| decimal(p,s) | Fixed precision and scale numbers. Allows numbers from $-10^{38} +1$ to $10^{38} -1$. The p parameter indicates the maximum total number of digits that can be stored (both to the left and to the right of the decimal point). p must be a value from 1 to 38. Default is 18. The s parameter indicates the maximum number of digits stored to the right of the decimal point. s must be a value from 0 to p. Default value is 0 | 5-17 bytes |
| numeric(p,s) | Fixed precision and scale numbers. Allows numbers from $-10^{38} +1$ to $10^{38} -1$. The p parameter indicates the maximum total number of digits that can be stored (both to the left and to the right of the decimal point). p must be a value from 1 to 38. Default is 18. The s parameter indicates the maximum number of digits stored to the right of the decimal point. s must be a value from 0 to p. Default value is 0 | 5-17 bytes |
| smallmoney | Monetary data from -214,748.3648 to 214,748.3647 | 4 bytes |
| money | Monetary data from -922,337,203,685,477.5808 to 922,337,203,685,477.5807 | 8 bytes |
| float(n) | Floating precision number data from -1.79E + 308 to 1.79E + 308. The n parameter indicates whether the field should hold 4 or 8 bytes. float(24) holds a 4-byte field and float(53) holds an 8-byte field. Default value of n is 53. | 4 or 8 bytes |
| real | Floating precision number data from -3.40E + 38 to 3.40E + 38 | 4 bytes |

## Date:

| Data type | Description | Storage |
|---|---|---|
| datetime | From January 1, 1753 to December 31, 9999 with an accuracy of 3.33 milliseconds | 8 bytes |
| datetime2 | From January 1, 0001 to December 31, 9999 with an accuracy of 100 nanoseconds | 6-8 bytes |
| smalldatetime | From January 1, 1900 to June 6, 2079 with an accuracy of 1 minute | 4 bytes |
| date | Store a date only. From January 1, 0001 to December 31, 9999 | 3 bytes |
| time | Store a time only to an accuracy of 100 nanoseconds | 3-5 bytes |
| datetimeoffset | The same as datetime2 with the addition of a time zone offset | 8-10 bytes |
| timestamp | Stores a unique number that gets updated every time a row gets created or modified. The timestamp value is based upon an internal clock and does not correspond to real time. Each table may have only one timestamp variable | |

## Other data types:

| Data type | Description |
|---|---|
| sql_variant | Stores up to 8,000 bytes of data of various data types, except text, ntext, and timestamp |
| uniqueidentifier | Stores a globally unique identifier (GUID) |
| xml | Stores XML formatted data. Maximum 2GB |
| cursor | Stores a reference to a cursor used for database operations |
| table | Stores a result-set for later processing |

# Conclusion

Thank you again for choosing this book!

I hope this book was able to help you to program like a pro using SQL.

The next step is to be diligent, practice, and apply your knowledge. Keep this book handy, as you will always find that the information within is a wonderful reference throughout your time programming with SQL.

Finally, if you enjoyed this book, then I'd like to ask you for a favor, would you be kind enough to leave a review for this book on Amazon? It'd be greatly appreciated!

Thank you and good luck!

# Other Books by Timothy Short

Linux: The Quick Start Beginners Guide

PowerShell: Beginner to Pro Guide

Blockchain: The Comprehensive Guide to Mastering the Hidden Economy

Raspberry Pi 3: Beginner to Pro Guide

WordPress: Beginner to Pro Guide

Shopify: Beginner to Pro Guide

Passive Income: The Ultimate Guide to Financial Freedom

Project Management: Beginner to Professional Manager and Respected Leader

Evernote: Made Simple: Master Time Management and Productivity

All available via amazon.com

Made in the USA
Lexington, KY
04 January 2017